Reading Grade 2

Best Value Books

P9-BJW-193

Table Of Contents

The student pages in this book have been specially prepared for reproduction on any standard copying machine.

Permission is hereby granted to the purchaser of this book to reproduce student pages for classroom use only. Reproduction for commercial resale or for an entire school or school system is strictly prohibited. No part of this book may be reproduced for storage in a retrieval system, or transmitted in any form, by any means (electronic, recording, mechanical, or otherwise) without the prior written permission of the publisher.

Kelley Wingate products are available at fine educational supply stores throughout the U. S. and Canada.

Reading Comprehension CD-3709   Printed in the United States Of America   ISBN 0-88724-427-0

Estimating Reading Ability

The following graded word lists may be used to estimate a student's reading grade level.

1. Ask the student to read each word in the list.

2. Keep count of the number of words the student reads from the list.

3. Estimate the student's ability to read materials at the same grade level as the grade level of the word list. Base your estimate upon:

23 or more   The student can probably read at this grade level without help.

18 - 22   The student can probably read at this grade level if given some help.

17 or less   The student can probably not read at this grade level even if given help.

1.	add	13.	lunchtime
2.	bar	14.	monkey
3.	board	15.	oil
4.	butter	16.	person
5	choose	17.	print
6.	cup	18.	ring
7.	drive	19.	seem
8.	extra	20.	signal
9.	foot	21.	spin
10.	growl	22.	super
11.	huge	23.	ticket
12.	knot	24.	untie
		25.	whisper

Ready-To-Use Ideas and Activities

The activities in this book will help children master the basic skills necessary to become competent learners. Remember as you read through the activities listed below, as you go through this book, that all children learn at their own rate. Although repetition is important, it is critical that we never lose sight of the fact that it is equally important to build children's self-esteem and self-confidence if we want them to become successful learners as well as good citizens.

If you are working with a child at home, try to set up a quiet comfortable environment where you will work. Make it a special time to which you each look forward. Do only a few activities at a time. Try to end each session on a positive note, and remember that fostering self-esteem and self-confidence is also critical to the learning process.

Story Comprehension

During or after story discussion, there are two different types of questions that you can ask to insure and enhance reading comprehension. The first type of question is a factual question. This type of question includes question words such as: who, what, when, where, and why. It can also include questions like How old is the character?, Where does the character live?, What time was it when....?, or any question that has a clear answer. The other type of question is an open-ended question. These questions will not have a clear answer. They are based on opinions about the story, not on facts. An open-ended question can be something like: Why do you think the character acted as he did?, How do you think the character felt about her actions or the actions of others?, What do you think the character will do next?, or What other ways could this story have ended?.

Flash card ideas

The back of this book has removable flash cards that will be great for use for basic skill and enrichment activities. Pull the flash cards out and either cut them apart or, if you have access to a paper cutter, use that to cut the flash cards apart.

The following are just a few ideas of ways you may want to use these flash cards:

Ready-To-Use Ideas and Activities

Write some or all of the flash card words on the chalkboard and divide the children into two or more groups. Now, as the children look over the list of words on the chalkboard, begin to describe any word from the list. Your description can be spelling characteristics, a definition, how the word makes you feel, whether it is a happy,sad, funny, or exciting word, or anything you can think of about the word. The team who guesses the word correctly first wins one point. After each word is guessed, correctly cross it off of the list and go on to another word. You can either have the group try and guess the correct word working together or you can have one person at a time from each group be the guesser.

Use some or all of the flash cards and write one sentence for each card containing a blank where the flash card word belongs. For example if the flash card word is "birthday", the sentence could be, Marsha just turned 8 and last week she had a _____ party. Now, divide the class into groups and hand out an equal number of sentences to each group. Also, give each group the flash cards that go with their sentences. Have each group complete the sentences by filling in the blank with the correct flash card word. Tell the students not to write on the sentences you have handed out. They should rewrite the sentences on another sheet of paper. After each group is finished you can check the sentences to make sure they are correct then have groups exchange the sentences with the blanks in them and the flash cards that go with them.

Reproduce the bingo sheet on the opposite page in this book, making enough to have one for each student. Hand them out to the students. Take the flash cards and write the words on the chalkboard. Have the students choose 24 of the words and write them in any order on the empty spaces of their bingo cards, writing only one word in each space. When all students have finished their cards, take the flash cards and make them into a deck. Call out the words one at a time. Any student who has a word that you call out should make an "X" through the word to cross it out. The student who crosses out five words in a row first (horizontally, vertically, or diagonally) wins the game. To extend the game you can continue playing until a student crosses out all of the words on his bingo sheet.

Vocabulary Bingo

		FREE		

©1995 Kelley Wingate Publications, Inc.

CD-3709

Name _____

1. Read the story

Kelly

Kelly takes off her shoes. She puts on her roller skates. Pull the laces tight, Kelly. You must tie them so the laces are not too long. Kelly stands up. She takes two tiny steps. Watch out!

2. Read the sentences below. Write them in order as they happened in the story.

_____

1.

_____

2.

_____

3.

_____

4.

_____

5.

_____

She puts on roller skates.

Kelly's shoes come off.

She stands up.

Kelly makes sure the laces are tight.

Kelly steps two times.

3. Draw a line under the best ending for this story.

Kelly takes off the skates.

Kelly falls down.

The roller skates need new laces.

1. Read the story.

Growing Flowers

Growing potted flowers is fun. Fill a pot with dirt. Plant seeds. Water them every day. Soon the stems and leaves will grow. Pull any weeds that come up. Buds will pop out in a few weeks.

2. Read the sentences below. Write them in order as they happened in the story.

Water the seeds.
Buds grow on the stems.
Put dirt in a pot.
Pull the weeds.
Plant the flower seeds.

1. _____

2. _____

3. _____

4. _____

5. _____

3. Draw a line under the best ending for this story.
Give the pot away.
Put the pot outside in the sun.
Flowers will bloom.

1. Read the story.

Fridays

Friday is the best day of all. Mom picks me up from school. Then, we get an ice cream cone. I like chocolate the best. We go to the park then have pizza for dinner. Sometimes we go to a movie.

2. Read the sentences below. Write them in order as they happened in the story.

1. _____

2. _____

3. _____

4. _____

5. _____

We have pizza for dinner.
I have chocolate ice cream.
We go to a movie.
Fridays are good days.
We play at the park.

3. Draw a line under the best ending for this story.
I am tired and go right to bed.
I do my homework.
Mom takes me back to school.

©1995 Kelley Wingate Publications, Inc.   CD-3709

1. Read the story.

Meyer and Tim

Meyer is a little boy. He has a puppy named Tim. Tim is also very young. Meyer and Tim are good friends. They play ball together. They take naps together. After their nap they share a snack.

2. Read the sentences below. Write them in order as they happened in the story.

1. _____

2. _____

3. _____

4. _____

5. _____

They are good friends.
They slept at the same time.
Meyer and Tim are both young.
They play ball together.
Meyer and Tim ate a snack.

3. Draw a line under the best ending for this story.
Meyer plays with another boy.
Tim eats a bone.
Tim sleeps all night on Meyer's bed.

1. Read the story.

Crossing the Street

It is important to be safe. Crossing a street the right way will help keep you safe. Walk to the corner. Stop at the curb. Look left and right. When there are no cars coming, it is safe to cross.

2. Read the sentences below. Write them in order as they happened in the story.

1. _____

2. _____

3. _____

4. _____

5. _____

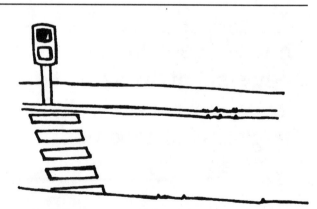

Cross when it is safe.
Look both ways for cars.
Crossing streets safely is important.
Stop at the corner.
Go to the corner.

3. Draw a line under the best ending for this story.
Wait for cars to come.
Look once more then walk across the street.
Quickly run across the street.

1. Read the story.

Mike

Mike loves to swing. He comes to the playground. It takes time to find the right swing. Mike sits down and pushes with his feet. He leans forward and backward. Look how high he goes!

2. Read the sentences below. Write them in order as they happened in the story.

1. _____

2. _____

3. _____

4. _____

5. _____

Mike pushes with his feet.
Mike swings very high.
He leans back and forth to make the swing go.
Mike goes to the playground.
He finds a swing that is just right.

3. Draw a line under the best ending for this story.
Mike swings until he is tired.
Mother calls Mike home.
He stops swinging and plays on the slide.

Name _____   skill: sequencing

1. Read the story.

Elly and the Cookie

    Mother baked cookies. She gave one to Elly. Oh, it smelled good! Elly took the cookie outside. She sat down to eat it. A little squirrel came up to Elly's foot. It looked hungry. Elly gave the squirrel a piece of cookie. Oh, it tasted good!

2. Read the sentences below. Write them in order as they happened in the story.

_____

1.

_____

2.

_____

3.

_____

4.

_____

5.

_____

She went outside to eat the cookie.
The cookie smelled good.
A squirrel came close to Elly.
She gave some cookie to the squirrel.
The squirrel looked hungry.

3. Draw a line under the best ending for this story.
Elly got angry with the squirrel.
The squirrel called his friends.
They both enjoyed the rest of the cookie.

1. Read the story.

Alyssa's Dance

Alyssa loves to dance for Mother. First, Alyssa stands on her toes. Then, she spins in circles. After that, she hops and leaps. Alyssa swings her arms over her head and bends to one side. Last, she bows to her mother.

2. Read the sentences below. Write them in order as they happened in the story.

_____

1. _____

2. _____

3. _____

4. _____

5. _____

Hopping and leaping comes next.
She sways her arms back and forth.
Alyssa bows low for her mother.
She stands on tip-toe then spins around.
Dancing is fun for Alyssa.

3. Draw a line under the best ending for this story.
Alyssa stands on her toes.
Alyssa goes to sleep
Mother claps and smiles.

1. Read the story.

Roger Rides His Bike

Roger can do tricks on his bike. In June he learned to ride very fast. In July he could ride while standing up. By August Roger could ride with no hands. I think he will ride without hands or feet soon! He learns very quickly.

2. Read the sentences in the box below. Write them in order as they happened in the story.

1. _____

2. _____

3. _____

4. _____

5. _____

He does not use his hands.
He might ride without using his feet.
Roger does tricks.
He rides quickly.
He can stand and ride the bike.

3. Draw a line under the best ending for this story.
Roger becomes a great bike rider.
Roger becomes a football player.
Roger sells his bike.

1. Read the story.

A Rock Collection

Collecting rocks is a fun hobby. First you must find some small rocks. Look for odd shapes or pretty colors. Wash away all the dirt. Put the rocks in a jar and cover them with water. Put a lid on the jar. The water makes the pretty colors brighter.

2. Read the sentences below. Write them in order as they happened in the story.

1. _____

2. _____

3. _____

4. _____

5. _____

Put the rocks into a jar.
Rock collecting is a fun hobby.
Cover the rocks with water.
Wash the rocks to get rid of the dirt.
Find some pretty or odd shaped rocks.

3. Draw a line under the best ending for this story.
Put the jar on a shelf so you can look at it.
Throw the rocks away.
Start a button collection.

Tina is very tiny. She is the smallest girl in her class. Her desk is big. The chalkboard is too high. But Tina is happy. She is very good at many things. She is a good reader.   She is a great speller. When she plays hide and seek, no one can find Tina!

1. **A good title for this story would be:**
   a. Hide and Seek
   b. Tiny Tina
   c. A Good Speller

2. **What two things are too big for Tina?**

   a. _____

   b. _____

3. **Why is Tina happy about herself?**

   a. _____

   b. _____

4. **What can Tina do better than most people?**

   _____

5. **Tell something else that a small person might be better at than a big person.**

   _____

Joey watched some children having a race. He wanted to join them, but he could not. Joey could not run. He could not walk. Joey had been in a wheelchair his whole life. The children saw Joey. They asked him if he would help them. They needed someone to decide who the winner of the race would be. Joey was pleased. Everyone had a good time.

BIG RACE TODAY

1. **A good title for this story would be:**
    a. The Race
    b. How Joey Helped
    c. A Wheelchair

2. **What did Joey want to do?**

_____

3. **Why couldn't Joey be in the race?**

_____

_____

4. **How did the children get Joey to play?**

_____

5. **How do you think Joey felt at the beginning of the story?**

_____

_____

Sunlight was shining from a silver sky. The weather was warming the woods. A baby bear was biting blueberries from a big bush. Bees buzzed in a bluebonnet bloom. Four frogs flicked fat flippers. Two turtles tucked in their tails. Spring season is special!

1. A good title for this story would be:
   a. Four Frogs in a Pond
   b. A Sunny Spring Day
   c. Baby Bear and the Blueberries

2. What was baby bear eating?

_____

3. Where were the bees?

_____

4. What is different about the words in this story?

_____

5. Write a sentence about Mary Mouse. Make most of the words begin with the letter "m".

_____

_____

A treehouse is a wonderful place to play. If you hide behind the leaves, no one will see you. Sit very still and you might see squirrels or birds playing in the tree. In a treehouse you can read a good book. You can daydream about what you will be someday. You can even pretend to be a pirate or an explorer. Ask a friend to come into your treehouse and you can have even more fun!

1. A good title for this story would be:
   a. A Treehouse
   b. Hiding in the Leaves
   c. A Good Way to Watch Birds

2. What are two things you can pretend to be in a treehouse?

_____

3. Why do you need to sit still to watch birds and squirrels?

_____

4. Why might you hide behind the leaves?

_____

5. What might you do with a friend in your treehouse?

_____

_____

I have a new baby sister. Her name is Amanda. Mom and Dad brought her home from the hospital last week. I want to play games with her but Mom says she is too little. She sleeps a lot. She cries a lot. She sure can't do much! She does like to watch me when she is awake. I hope she gets bigger soon.

1. A good title for this story would be:
   a. Growing Up
   b. Babies
   c. My Sister Amanda

2. When did Amanda come home?

_____

3. What are two things that Amanda can do?

a. _____

b. _____

4. Why do I want Amanda to get bigger soon?

_____

5. What are two things you can do with a new baby?

a. _____

b. _____

I went shopping with Dad last week. We walked past many rows of toys. I stopped to look at one toy that I really wanted to buy. When I looked up, Dad was gone! I did not move, but looked as far as I could see down the aisle. Dad was not there. I knew he was lost! "Dad?" I called. He came from around the corner. Dad was not lost anymore.

1. A good title for this story would be:
   a. Shopping with Dad
   b. Lost!
   c. Finding a Toy

2. What did I stop to look at?

---

3. A word that means "row" or "pathway" is:
   a. corner
   b. store
   c. aisle

4. What did I do to try and find Dad?

a. _____

b. _____

5. Was it really Dad or the child who was lost? Explain.

_____

_____

Dorothy got a box of magic tricks for her birthday. She learned how to change one coin into another. She learned how to make two pieces of rope turn into one piece of rope. Dorothy put on a magic show for her friends. They liked her tricks very much. The magic box was Dorothy's favorite birthday present.

1. **A good title for this story would be:**
   a. Dorothy's Magic Box
   b. The Best Birthday
   c. Dorothy Puts on a Show

2. **What could she do with two pieces of rope?**

_____

3. **How did Dorothy's friends feel about her show?**

_____

4. **What is another word for "favorite"?**
   a. best loved
   b. worst
   c. easy to use

5. **Which trick would you like to learn to do? Why?**

_____

_____

Chuck lives in the country. He has a big barn and a lot of land, but no animals. Chuck does not grow animals. He grows trees. Chuck has many kinds of fruit trees. He grows pear, apple, cherry, and plum trees. Each spring and fall he is busy picking their fruit. It is fun to go to Chuck's farm when the fruit is ripe. Yum, yum!

1. A good title for this story would be:
   a. Fruit Tastes Good
   b. Many Trees
   c. Chuck's Fruit Farm

2. Why doesn't Chuck have animals?

_____

3. What four kinds of fruit does Chuck grow?

_____

_____

4. The word "ripe" means:
   a. growing
   b. ready to pick
   c. red

5. Name two other fruits that grow on trees.
   a. _____

   b. _____

There is a new boy in our class. His name is Brian. Today is his first day at our school. He rode to school on my bus. He was very quiet at lunch. He stood near the wall and did not play during recess. I think he might be nice because he smiled whenever I looked at him. He might just be bashful. Do you think we could become friends?

1. A good title for this story would be:
    a. A New Boy
    b. Brian is quiet
    c. My Friend

2. What two things does Brian do that show me he is bashful?

    a. _____

    b. _____

3. What makes me think Brian is nice?

_____

4. What word means the same as "bashful"?
    a. shy
    b. loud
    c. unfriendly

5. What can I do to become friends with the new boy?

_____

Joe is the man who lives next door. Mother says he is pretty old, but I don't think so. Joe is always in his yard when I come home from school. He invites me to sit on the front steps with him. He listens to me as I tell him about my day at school. He tells wonderful stories that make me laugh and laugh. Joe may be old in years, but he is my best friend!

1. A good title for this story would be:
   a. Joe Tells Stories
   b. An Old Man
   c. My Friend Joe

2. What does Mother think about Joe?

_____

3. What two things make me like Joe so much?

a. _____

b. _____

4. Another word for "invite" is:
   a. tell
   b. ask
   c. pick

5. What other things can older people and children enjoy together?

_____

Parts of The Body

Your body has many parts. Some parts protect you, or keep you safe. Your skin covers your body. It protects the things inside you. Some body parts help you learn about things. They are called your senses. Your eyes let you see what is around you. You listen with your ears. You learn smells by using your nose. Your mouth lets you taste things. Skin helps you learn how things feel. All of these parts are on the outside of your body.

1. **What is the main idea of this story?**
   a. Your body has many parts.
   b. Skin protects other parts inside your body.
   c. We learn by using our eyes.

2. **Name six parts of your body.**

   _____

3. **The word protect means:**
   a. feel
   b. skin
   c. keep safe

4. **What does skin do?**

   _____

5. **What outside body parts help you learn?**

   _____

6. **How do body parts help you learn?**

   _____

Inside The Body

Many body parts cannot be seen because they are inside the body. Bones and muscles are inside your body. Some body parts are called organs. Organs are body parts that do special jobs. Your brain, heart, and lungs are organs. They do special jobs that help you. Your brain helps you think. Your heart pumps your blood. Your lungs help you breathe. You do not have to think about making them work. They do their jobs automatically, without you telling them.

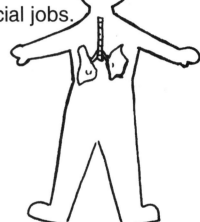

1. What is the main idea of this story?
    a. Organs are parts inside your body that do special jobs.
    b. You do not have to tell organs to do their jobs.
    c. Some parts are inside the body.
2. The word "organ" means:
    a. to think about
    b. bones and muscles
    c. body parts that do special jobs
3. Name three organs.

_____

_____

4. "Automatically" means:
    a. without thinking about it
    b. thinking about something
    c. organs
5. Why can't you see some of your body parts?

_____

6. Which body part pumps your blood?

_____

Think about it: Make a list of all the inside body parts you can name. Try to think of what job each part does.

Heart

Your heart is an organ inside your chest. The heart is a muscle about the size of your fist. It works all the time without you thinking about it. Every time your heart beats, it pushes blood into your body. The blood goes to every part of your body (from head to toe) then comes back to the heart. This organ works harder than any other muscle you have. It works while you are awake or asleep. It works harder while you run or play. The heart never stops to rest!

1. **What is the main idea of this story?**
   a. The heart never stops.
   b. Blood goes to every part of a body.
   c. The heart is an organ.
2. **How big is a heart?**

_____

3. **Where is your heart?**

_____

4. **What job does the heart do?**

_____

5. **What is the heart made of?**

_____

6. **When does the heart work very hard?**

_____

Think about it: Find your heartbeat by putting your two middle fingers against your neck just under your jaw. Count the number of times your heart beats in one minute.

Lungs

You have two organs called lungs inside your chest. There is one on each side of your heart. Your lungs bring air into your body. As you breathe, or take in air, your chest gets bigger. That is because your lungs are filling with air. Their job is to take a gas called oxygen out of the air. Your body uses oxygen. You need it to live. Lungs get the oxygen from the air then send it to the rest of your body.

1. **What is the main idea of this story?**
    a. Lungs take oxygen from the air.
    b. Your chest gets bigger as you breathe in.
    c. Lungs are organs near your heart.
2. **Where inside your body will you find the lungs?**

_____

3. **The word "breathe" means:**
    a. live
    b. take in air
    c. lungs
4. **What is oxygen?**

_____

5. **Why does your chest get bigger when you breathe?**

_____

6. **What happens to the oxygen in your lungs?**

_____

_____

Think about it: Why do you think you need to take in new air every few seconds?

Name _____

Stomach

You eat food every day. The food you eat becomes energy for your body. You put the food into your mouth. Chewing helps break the food into smaller pieces. As you swallow, the food passes into your stomach. The stomach is an organ in the middle of your body. It is just below the heart and lungs. When food reaches the stomach it is broken into even smaller pieces. Some of the pieces are used to make energy for your body. The blood picks up these pieces and takes them to the rest of your body.

1. **What is the main idea of this story?**
   a. You must eat food to stay alive.
   b. Food is changed into energy.
   c. The stomach is an organ that changes food to help make energy.
2. **What does chewing do to food?**

_____

3. **How does food get to your stomach?**

_____

4. **What happens to food in your stomach?**

_____

5. **How do the pieces of food get to other parts of the body?**

_____

6. **Why do we need to eat?**

_____

_____

Think about it: How do you think your teeth help your stomach?

Brain

Your brain is a very important organ inside your head. Your brain is where all thinking and learning takes place. The brain gets information, or facts, from your senses (eyes, ears, nose, mouth, and skin). Your brain tells your body what to do. When your ears hear someone call your name they send the sound to your brain. Your brain tells you to answer. Your brain also takes care of things you don't think about. It tells your lungs to breathe and your heart to beat. Your brain controls everything you do.

1. **What is the main idea of this story?**
   a. Your brain controls your body.
   b. The brain tells your heart to beat.
   c. The brain is an organ.
2. **Where is your brain?**

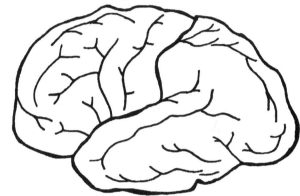

_____

3. **The word "information" means:**
   a. brain
   b. control
   c. facts
4. **Where does the brain get information?**

_____

5. **What are the five senses?**

_____

6. **Why don't you have to think about breathing?**

_____

_____

Think about it: What are other things your body does automatically?

Working Together

Each part of your body has a job to do. All the parts work together to help each other. The blood goes to every part of the body. It carries things your body needs. The blood gets oxygen in the lungs. It gets food in the stomach. It takes the food and oxygen to all the parts of your body. The brain gets food and oxygen through the blood. Food and oxygen help the brain work. The brain tells all the parts what to do. It makes sure all the parts work together. All the parts working together keep you alive and healthy, or well.

1. **What is the main idea of this story?**
   a. Each part of your body has a job.
   b. Body parts work together to keep us alive.
   c. Blood takes food to the rest of the body.

2. **How does the heart work with the stomach?**

_____

3. **How do the lungs work with the stomach?**

_____

4. **The word "healthy" means:**
   a. well, not sick
   b. alive
   c. working together

5. **How do the stomach and lungs help the brain?**

_____

6. **How does the brain help other parts of the body?**

_____

_____

Think about it: What would happen if any one body part does not do its job?

Staying Healthy

Your body works for you. It works to keep you alive and healthy. You must take care of your body so it can do its job. There are things you can do to help your body stay strong and healthy. You can exercise, drink water, eat good foods, and rest. Doing these things helps keep your body strong.   Eating and drinking gives your body energy to do its job. Exercising and resting helps keep your body strong. When you do good things for your body, it is able to do the things you want it to. It is important to take care of your body.

1. **What is the main idea of this story?**
   a. You need to take care of your body.
   b. You must exercise.
   c. Resting is important.
2. **Name four things you should do for your body.**

_____

_____

3. **What does your body do for you?**

_____

4. **Why should you take care of your body?**

_____

5. **Why should you eat good foods?**

_____

_____

Think about it: What might happen to your body if you did not take care of it?

Exercise and Rest

Exercise is one thing you can do to stay healthy. Muscles need to be used or they will become weak (not strong). Running, playing, and working helps make your muscles stronger. The more you use muscles, the stronger they will be. It is also important to get enough rest. As you exercise or use your muscles, you use energy. Resting gives your body a chance to relax and gather new energy. Children need even more sleep than grown-ups. Children are growing every day, and growing takes a lot of energy. You need to work and play every day. Be sure to get enough sleep, too!

1. **What is the main idea of this story?**
    a. Exercising makes muscles strong.
    b. It is important to get enough exercise and rest.
    c. Children need more rest than adults.
2. **What are some ways to make your muscles strong?**

_____

3. **The word "weak" means:**
    a. exercise
    b. sleep
    c. not strong
4. **How does exercise help you stay healthy?**

_____

5. **How does resting help your body?**

_____

6. **Why do children need more sleep than grown-ups?**

_____

Think about it: Keep a list of things you do today that help make your muscles strong.

Germs

One thing you can do to help your body stay healthy is to keep yourself clean. You should wash your hands before you eat. You should take a bath every day and keep your hair clean. You should keep your teeth clean by brushing them after you eat. Keeping your body clean is very important. Washing and being clean helps keep germs away. Germs are tiny little living things that you cannot see. They are in the air and on things we touch. Some germs can make you sick when they get inside your body. Keeping yourself clean helps kill germs and keeps you healthy.

1. **What is the main idea of this story?**
   a. Take a bath every day.
   b. Germs can make you sick.
   c. Keeping clean can kill germs that make you sick.
2. **How can you keep your teeth clean?**

_____

3. **What is a "germ"?**
   a. air
   b. tiny living things
   c. dirt
4. **Why is it important to keep yourself clean?**

_____

5. **How can germs hurt you?**

_____

6. **How can you keep yourself clean?**

_____

_____

Think about it: Keep a list of things you do today that keep you clean.

Clothing

One way to help keep your body healthy is to wear the right clothes. You do not wear a heavy coat in the summer. You do not wear shorts in the winter. Your body needs to stay at the right temperature, or amount of heat. Wearing the right clothes helps keep you just the right temperature. During the summer when it is hot, we wear light clothes that let the heat escape, or get away from our body. During cold weather we wear hats, coats, and long pants that keep the heat in our bodies. Umbrellas and raincoats also help us. They keep our bodies dry. Getting wet cools our bodies. We wear rain clothes to help keep us warm and dry in wet weather. If we get too hot or too cold, our bodies have a hard time doing their jobs.

1. **What is the main idea of this story?**
   a. It is important to wear the right clothes.
   b. We wear shorts in the summer.
   c. Raincoats keep us dry.
2. **A word that means "amount of heat" is:**
   a. clothes
   b. temperature
   c. escape
3. **What warm things should we wear in the winter?**

_____

4. **Another word for "escape" is:**
   a. get away
   b. temperature
   c. dry
5. **Why do we wear cool clothes in the summer?**

_____

6. **What happens if your body is too warm or too cold?**

_____

Think about it: Draw a picture of yourself in winter and one in summer.

Food

Eating the right food is very important in keeping your body healthy. Your body uses food to make energy. Some foods are better for making energy than other foods. These good foods have things your body needs to grow strong and healthy. The Food Pyramid helps you choose good foods to eat. Dairy foods like milk and cheese are good for your bones and teeth. Meat and beans help build muscle. Fruits and vegetables give your body vitamins. Bread,cereal, rice, and pasta help give your body energy that will last a long time. A healthy meal will have foods from each of these pyramind groups.

1. **What is the main idea of this story?**
   a. Eating is fun.
   b. Milk helps your bones and teeth.
   c. Foods from the Food Pyramid give your body the things it needs to stay healthy.

2. **Why do you need to eat good foods?**

_____

3. **Name foods from the Food Pyramid.**

_____

_____

4. **What kind of food helps muscles?**

_____

5. **What do fruits and vegetable give your body?**

_____

Taking Care of Your Teeth

Your teeth are very important to your health. Without strong teeth you cannot eat the foods that your body needs. Food can get stuck between your teeth. Sugar coats your teeth. The food and sugar can put holes called cavities in your teeth. You should brush your teeth every morning and every night. Brushing well gets food and sugar off your teeth. Two times a year you should visit your dentist, a doctor who takes care of teeth. The dentist will clean your teeth and fill any cavities you might have.

1. **What is the main idea of this story?**
    a. Teeth help us eat.
    b. It is important to take care of your teeth.
    c. A dentist checks your teeth.
2. **Why do we need strong healthy teeth?**

    _____

3. **The word "cavity" means:**
    a. a hole in a tooth
    b. a doctor
    c. strong teeth
4. **What can give you cavities?**

    _____

5. **What can you do to keep your teeth healthy?**

    _____

6. **How do dentists help our teeth?**

    _____

Think about it: Count how many teeth you have. How many fillings do your have (cavities that have been fixed)? Compare your answers with other people in the class.

Checkups

Each year you should visit your doctor for a checkup. A checkup is when the doctor sees how well you are growing. The doctor will see how much weight you have gained. She will measure how tall you are to make sure you are growing as you should. The doctor will check many parts of your body. She will look in your ears and listen to your heart to see if you have any health problems. A checkup can help the doctor find any problems that may be beginning. A checkup makes sure that you stay healthy!

1. **What is the main idea of this story?**
    a. A checkup keeps you healthy.
    b. The doctor checks your weight.
    c. The doctor may find problems that are beginning.

2. **How many times a year should you have a checkup?**

_____

3. **What is a checkup?**

_____

4. **How can the doctor tell if you are growing as you should?**

_____

5. **What will the doctor do to you during a checkup?**

_____

6. **What is the doctor looking for during a checkup?**

_____

Think about it: Find out when your last checkup was.

Medicine

Sometimes you go to the doctor when you are sick. The doctor tells you what is wrong. She gives you medicine, something that helps make you well. The medicine can be a shot, pills, or something you drink. No one likes to take medicine, but it helps make you healthy again. Sometimes during a checkup the doctor will give you medicine that helps keep you from getting sick. This medicine is called a vaccine. A vaccine can keep you from getting measles, mumps, and other illnesses. Taking medicine when you need it will help you get better. Taking good care of your body all the time will help you stay healthy.

1. **What is the main idea of this story?**
   a. Medicine helps make you healthy.
   b. No one likes to take medicine.
   c. Some medicines keep you from getting sick.
2. **"Medicine" is:**
   a. a shot
   b. something that makes you feel better when you are sick
   c. illness
3. **Name three ways you can take medicine.**

   _____

4. **A word that means "medicine that keeps you healthy" is:**
   a. vaccine
   b. measles
   c. illness
5. **Why do doctors give you vaccines?**

   _____

6. **Why do we take medicine?**

   _____

Think about it: If you take care of yourself and get vaccines will you ever get sick? Explain what you think and why.

Animals

Animals are living things that can move and reproduce, or make new animals. There are many kinds of animals. Man is an animal. Birds are animals. A snail is an animal. Even bees and ants are animals. All animals need to eat. They eat plants or other animals to give them energy, or strength. All animals need to be safe. They build homes to protect themselves from weather and other animals.

1. **What is the main idea of this story?**
    a. Man is an animal.
    b. Animals build homes.
    c. Animals are living things.
2. **Name four animals.**

_____

_____

3. **The word reproduce means:**
    a. animals
    b. make new animals
    c. keep safe
4. **Another word for energy is:**
    a. strength
    b. protect
    c. snail
5. **Why do animals need to eat?**

_____

6. **Why do animals need to build homes?**

_____

Think about it: Can you name four animals that are not in this story?

Extinct

Many kinds of animals are extinct, all of their kind have died. Dinosaurs are extinct. There are no more dinosaurs alive on the earth. Scientists, people who study nature, are not sure what killed them. Some animals are extinct because the land where they lived changed. Others are extinct because hunters killed too many of them. When an animal becomes extinct it is gone forever.

1. **What is the main idea of this story?**
   a. Some animals are extinct.
   b. Dinosaurs are extinct.
   c. Hunters kill animals.
2. **Why are dinosaurs extinct?**

_____

3. **The word "extinct" means:**
   a. all of those animals are dead
   b. not sure
   c. almost all of those animals are dead
4. **A word that means "people who study the earth" is:**
   a. extinct
   b. nature
   c. scientist
5. **What two things can make an animal extinct?**

_____

6. **How can we get extinct animals to come back?**

_____

_____

Think about it: What can we do to make sure no more animals become extinct?

Endangered

Some kinds of animals are in trouble. There are not many left and they may become extinct. These animals are endangered, or in danger of becoming extinct. The bald eagles are endangered. They were hunted for many years. The panda is another endangered animal. It lives in the forests of China. Many of the forests have been cleared, or cut for the wood and land. Now the pandas have less space and less food. Some people are trying to help endangered animals. There are laws to keep endangered animals safe.

1. What is the main idea of this story?
   a. Pandas live in China.
   b. Some animals are close to being extinct.
   c. Laws help endangered animals.

2. A word that means "in danger of becoming extinct" is:
   a. extinct
   b. endangered
   c. panda

3. Why are bald eagles endangered?

4. Another word for cleared is:
   a. cut down
   b. space
   c. land

5. Why is the panda endangered?

_____

6. What are people doing to help endangered animals?

_____

Think about it: How can we help endangered animals?

Name _____ skill: comprehension

Plants

Plants are living things. They can grow and reproduce. Most plants grow from seeds. When the plant gets big it makes new seeds. It is called a parent plant. A nut is a seed. A flower makes seeds. A seed needs three things to grow. It needs water, air, and a warm place to grow. Most seeds are planted in the spring. It is warm in the spring, and there is more water in the soil.

1. **What is the main idea of this story?**
   a. Plants are living things.
   b. A flower makes seeds.
   c. It is warm in the spring.
2. **How do new plants start?**

_____

3. **What is a parent plant?**

_____

4. **What is a seed?**

_____

5. **What three things do seeds need to begin growing?**

_____

_____

6. **When are most seeds planted?**

_____

Think about it: Name three things that have seeds.

How Seeds Grow

A new plant grows from a seed. The seed has a tough, or hard, outside part called the seed coat. Inside the seed coat is the new plant. There is also food for the new plant stored inside the seed coat. As the new plant eats the stored food and begins to grow, the seed coat splits so the plant can come out. A tiny new plant is called a seedling. It looks like its parent plant, but is much smaller. When it uses up all the stored food, the seedling will make its own food. Seedlings make their food from water, air, and light.

1. **What is the main idea of this story?**
   a. New plants look like the parent plant.
   b. The seed coat protects the new plant.
   c. Seeds grow into seedlings.
2. **A word that means hard is:**
   a. split
   b. stored
   c. tough
3. **What is a seed coat?**

_____

4. **A new plant is called a:**
   a. seed coat
   b. seedling
   c. split
5. **What is inside a seed coat?**

_____

6. **What do seedlings need to make their own food?**

_____

Think about it: Open an apple or orange seed. Find the seed coat, stored food, and new plant inside.

Parts of a Plant

Most plants have roots, stems, and leaves. Each part helps the plant in a special way. Roots are under the soil. They hold the plant so it can grow. Roots get water from the soil and give it to the plant. Stems are the body of the plant. They can be tall or short, hard or soft. Stems hold the leaves up to get light. They carry water from the roots to the leaves. Leaves make the food for the plant. They use air and light to make food. All three parts are important to plants.

1. **What is the main idea of this story?**
   a. Plants have three parts.
   b. Leaves make food for the plant.
   c. Roots hold the plant up.
2. **What do roots do?**

_____

3. **Which part of a plant holds up the leaves?**
   a. roots
   b. stem
   c. leaves
4. **What does the stem do?**

_____

5. **What do the leaves do?**

_____

6. **Why does a plant need all three parts?**

_____

Think about it: Draw a picture of a plant. Label the roots, stem, and leaves.

How We Use Plants

People need plants. Trees give us wood that we use to build things.
Trees also give us shade and help us stay cool in warm weather. People
eat many kinds of plants. We eat some roots. Onions, beets, and carrots
are plant roots. We eat stems. Celery is a plant stem. We eat leaves.
Spinach and lettuce are plant leaves. We also eat seeds. Nuts and berries
are plant seeds. When we eat these plant parts, we are getting the food the
plant has stored for itself.

1. **What is the main idea of this story?**
    a. Trees help us in many ways.
    b. Plant parts taste good.
    c. People use plants in many ways.

2. **How do trees help us?**

_____

3. **What parts of plants do we eat?**

_____

4. **Name three roots that we eat.**

_____

_____

5. **Name two kinds of leaves that we eat.**

_____

6. **What do we get when we eat plants?**

_____

Think about it: Make a list of foods we get from plant roots, stems,
leaves, and seeds.

Name _____ skill: comprehension

Flowers and Fruit

Most plants have flowers that make their seeds. The flower petals come in many shapes and bright colors. Some flowers are tiny and hard to find. Others are very large and pretty. The seeds of these plants are made inside the flowers. When the seeds are ready, the petals dry up and fall off. The part of the flower that holds the seeds gets bigger. This part grows and becomes the fruit. Apples and oranges are fruits that grow from flowers. The fruit has the plant seeds inside.

1. **What is the main idea of this story?**
    a. Many seeds come from plant flowers.
    b. Many plants have flowers.
    c. Fruit has seeds.

2. **What do flowers make?**

_____

3. **What color and shape are flower petals?**

_____

4. **What happens to the flower when the seeds are ready?**

_____

5. **What is inside the fruit?**

_____

6. **Name two kinds of fruit.**

_____

_____

Think about it: Can you name three other kinds of fruit?

Nuts and Cones

Some plants do not have flowers or fruit. They have nuts or cones to make new seeds. Walnuts, acorns, and almonds are nuts. The new plant and its stored food are inside a hard shell. As the seed begins to grow, the shell cracks open so the new plant can get bigger. Other plants, like the pine tree, have cones that hold their seeds. Cones are hard on the outside. The hard cone keeps the seeds safe inside. There are many seeds inside one cone. When the seeds are ready, the cone opens and they fall out.

1. **What is the main idea of this story?**
    a. A pine tree has seeds in a cone.
    b. Some plants have seeds inside nuts or cones.
    c. Some plants do not have flowers or fruit.

2. **What are the three parts of a nut?**

    _____

3. **How does the new plant get out of a nut?**

    _____

4. **What is inside a pine cone?**

    _____

5. **What happens when a cone opens?**

    _____

6. **Name three kinds of nuts that are seeds for plants.**

    _____

    _____

Think about it: Make a list of plants that have nuts or cones for seeds.

How Seeds Travel

A parent plant makes a lot of seeds. The seeds must leave the parent and get into the soil before they can grow. Some seeds just drop from the parent plant. Other seeds travel, or go far away, before they grow. The wind carries some kinds of seeds. Other seeds are sticky or have hooks that help them stick to animals that pass by. The animal may carry the seeds a long way before they fall off and find their way into the soil. Some seeds can float, or ride on top of water. The water carries these seeds far from the parent plant before they find a place to grow. Only a few seeds will grow. Many never find a place that has enough water or light. Others are eaten by animals. If every seed found a place to grow, the world would have too many plants!

1. **What is the main idea of this story?**
   a. Seeds must find a good place to grow.
   b. The wind carries some seeds to new places.
   c. Animals eat many seeds.
2. **Name three ways that seeds can travel.**

_____

3. **A word that means "to stay on top of water" is:**
   a. seed
   b. travel
   c. float
4. **How do animals help seeds?**

_____

5. **How do animals stop seeds from growing?**

_____

Think about it: What would happen if every seed found a place to grow?

Matter

Plants take up space. Animals take up space. Nonliving things, things that are not alive, take up space, too. Things that take up space are called matter. Look around your room. Can you see matter? The desks are matter. The books are matter. Even the teacher is matter! Matter can be put into three groups. They are called states of matter, or kinds of matter. These states are solid, liquid, and gas. All matter is in one of these states. Some matter can change from one state to another. Water is matter that can be in any of the states. Water is a liquid. When it is frozen it becomes a solid. When water becomes very hot it turns into steam, which is a gas. All three states take up space. All three states are forms of matter.

1. What is the main idea of this story?
   a. Water is liquid matter.
   b. Matter is anything that takes up space.
   c. Gas is matter.

2. What is matter?

_____

3. A word that means "not alive" is:
   a. nonliving
   b. matter
   c. states of matter

4. Another word for "states" is:
   a. kinds
   b. nonliving
   c. liquid

5. What are the three states of matter?

_____

_____

Think about it: Make a list of kinds of matter you can find in your classroom.

Volume and Mass

Which takes up more space, an ant or a table? The table does because it is bigger than the ant. The size of the space something takes up is called volume. Things that take up space can be heavy or light. An elephant is heavy. A piece of paper that is taller than the elephant is light. The elephant has more mass. Mass is the amount of matter something has. Think of two boxes that are the same size. One box is filled with feathers. The other box is filled with books. They both have the same volume, or size. The box with the books is heavier. It has more mass than the box with the feathers.

1. **What is the main idea of this story?**
    a. Things can be heavy or light.
    b. Books are heavier than feathers.
    c. Matter has volume and mass.
2. **A word that means "the amount of space taken" is:**
    a. mass
    b. volume
    c. heavy
3. **Are bigger things always heavier than smaller things?**

_____

4. **What does the word "mass" mean?**
    a. the size of something
    b. feathers
    c. the amount of matter something has
5. **Which has more volume, a pencil or a book?**

_____

6. **Which has more mass, a gallon of water or a gallon of air?**

_____

Think about it: Make a list of things that have a lot of volume, but not much mass.

Solid

There are three kinds of matter. They are called solid, liquid, and gas. Solid matter will keep its shape even when it is moved. A pencil is solid. It looks the same on your desk or in your hand. It does not change its shape. Solids can be soft, too. A shirt is a soft solid. It can bend and move with you, but it does not change its shape. The shirt will never look like a box or a ball. It will always have the shape of a shirt. A solid will have the same shape, volume, and mass any place you put it. It does not change by itself.

1. **What is the main idea of this story?**
    a. Solid matter does not change from place to place.
    b. A pencil is a solid.
    c. A shirt is a soft solid.

2. **What happens to a solid's shape when you move it?**

_____

3. **Circle the things in the list below that are solid matter.**

cup	water	book	chair
doll	tree	milk	bread
coat	car	person	juice

4. **What three things will stay the same anywhere the solid matter goes?**

_____

_____

5. **Are all solids hard? Explain.**

_____

_____

Think about it: Make a list of solid matter you can find in your classroom.

Liquid

One kind of matter is liquid. Liquid matter does not have a shape at all. Water is a liquid. It does not have its own shape. It will take the shape of whatever you put it in. Measure one cup of water and pour it into a tall glass. The water now has the shape of the glass. If you pour that water into a bowl, it spreads out and takes the shape of the bowl. The amount of water, or volume, has not changed. You had one cup in the glass and the same cup of water in the bowl. The shape of the water did change. A liquid will change its shape when it is moved, but it does not change volume or mass. It will be the same amount and weight no matter where you put it.

1. **What is the main idea of this story?**
     a. Liquid is a matter that changes shape.
     b. Water is a liquid.
     c. Liquids are a kind of matter.
2. **What is a liquid?**

_____

3. **What happens to water when you move it from one place to another?**

_____

4. **Circle the things in the list below that are liquid matter .**

cup	water	book	tea
doll	tree	milk	bread
cola	car	person	juice

5. **What stays the same when a liquid is moved?**

_____

Think about it: Make a list of liquid matter you can find in your home or classroom.

Gas

The third kind of matter is called gas. Gas, like liquid, does not have a shape. Air is a gas. It takes the shape of whatever you put it in. Blow air into a balloon. The air takes the shape of the balloon. Put air into a bicycle tire. It takes the shape of the tire. Gas can change its volume, or size, too. If you put the balloon in a cool place over night, it will be smaller in the morning. The air did not leak out. It became smaller! The air can expand, or get bigger, if it is warmed. Gas does not have a shape and it can change its volume.

1. **What is the main idea of this story?**
    a. Air will take the shape of a balloon.
    b. Gas is a type of matter.
    c. Gas has no shape.

2. **What happens to a gas when you move it to a new place?**

_____

3. **What happens to a gas if it is heated or cooled?**

_____

4. **What word means "to get bigger"?**
    a. gas
    b. leak
    c. expand

5. **How is gas different from solid?**

_____

6. **How is gas different from liquid?**

_____

Think about it: Make a chart that tells about solids, liquids, and gases. List things that belong to each group.

Community

People live together in groups. They help each other every day. We live in towns or cities where people help each other by doing their jobs. We do not grow our own food. We do not make our own clothes. Other people have the jobs of getting food and clothes in their stores so we can buy them. These types of jobs give us goods, or products we need. Other people have service jobs. These people do things we do not have time to do ourselves. People who mow lawns, clean clothes, or cut hair provide services. When people live near each other and help each other they are called a community. The town or city where you live is a community.

1. **What is the main idea of this story?**
   a. The grocer gives us food.
   b. We live in communities to help each other.
   c. Some jobs give a service.
2. **Why do we live in communities?**

_____

3. **Another word for goods is:**
   a. products
   b. services
   c. nice people
4. **Another word for service is:**
   a. watch
   b. important
   c. do things for others

5. **Why do people need to help each other?**

_____

6. **What is a community?**

_____

Think about it: Can you name three other service jobs?

©1995 Kelley Wingate Publications, Inc.   55   CD-3709

Police

One service job we see almost every day is a policeman. The police in our community have many jobs to do. They watch the roads to see that people drive safely. They give tickets if we drive too fast or break the rules of the road. Police also look for people who are breaking other laws. They try to protect us from robbers and other bad people. Police also help in other ways. If we get lost they can help us find our way home. Police make sure that people obey the laws that keep us safe.

1. **What is the main idea of this story?**
   a. Police give tickets.
   b. Police help lost people.
   c. Police have service jobs.

2. **Why do police watch the roads?**

_____

3. **Another word for protect is:**
   a. keep us safe
   b. hide
   c. stop

4. **How can police help us?**

_____

5. **What do police do if someone drives too fast?**

_____

6. **What is another word for obey?**
   a. drive safely
   b. follow the rules
   c. keep safe

Think about it: Can you name three other service jobs?

©1995 Kelley Wingate Publications, Inc.   CD-3709

Name _____   skill: comprehension

Firefighters

One service job we all know is the firefighter. The firefighter drives a big red truck. A firefighter wears a large hat and a heavy coat. A firefighter's job is to put out fires. In big cities the firefighters live in the firehouse so they are ready to go at all times. They take turns cooking dinner and keeping the firehouse clean. In some towns the firefighters are volunteers. They are usually not paid and do the job because they want to help. They have other jobs and are firefighters only when there is a fire. When an alarm sounds, these firefighters leave their jobs and go to the firehouse. Both kinds of firefighters help keep our homes and businesses safe.

1. **What is the main idea of this story?**
    a. Firefighters work in the city.
    b. Firefighters are ready anytime.
    c. Firefighters help protect us from fires.
2. **What does a firefighter do?**

_____

3. **What does a firefighter wear?**

_____

4. **Where do big city firefighters live?**

_____

5. **What does volunteer mean?**
    a. not paid for work
    b. firehouse
    c. has another job
6. **How do volunteer firefighters know when there is a fire?**

_____

Think about it: Why do city firefighters need to live at the firehouse?

Doctor

A doctor helps people who are sick or hurt. Doctors go to school for many years to learn how our bodies work. They study many subjects and work in hospitals to learn how to make people well. Some doctors specialize, or become an expert, in one thing. They may take care of just hearts, eyes, bones, or other parts of the body. Doctors also learn about medicine or drugs. They know what to give us to help make us well again. Doctors are an important part of our community. They help to keep all of us well.

1. **What is the main idea of this story?**
   a. Doctors keep us well.
   b. Some doctors take care of hearts.
   c. Doctors learn about medicine.
2. **What do doctors learn about in school?**

_____

3. **What is a doctor's job?**

_____

4. **What is a word that means specialize?**
   a. to be important
   b. teach
   c. become an expert
5. **What is a word that means drugs?**
   a. specialize
   b. medicine
   c. body
6. **Why are doctors important to a community?**

_____

_____

Think about it: Why might you go to see a doctor?

Dentist

Sometimes people have a problem with their teeth. They may get a cavity in their tooth. A cavity is a hole that can be painful if it is not taken care of. Special doctors called dentists take care of our teeth. We should see a dentist two times each year. The dentist will clean our teeth and look for problems during this checkup. This helps keep our teeth and gums healthy. If you have a toothache or cavity, the dentist can fix the problem. As people get older they may lose some teeth. A dentist can make false teeth called dentures for them to wear. A dentist has the job of keeping our teeth clean and healthy.

1. **What is the main idea of this story?**
    a. Dentists fill cavities.
    b. Dentists make dentures.
    c. Dentists keep our teeth clean and healthy.
2. **Another word for a hole in your tooth is:**
    a. denture
    b. cavity
    c. dentist
3. **Why should we visit the dentist twice a year?**

_____

4. **Name two things a dentist can help you with.**

_____

_____

5. **How does a dentist help our community?**

_____

_____

Think about it: Tell about the last time you went to see your dentist.

Farmer

Farmers are a part of a community. Most people do not have enough time to grow their own food. A farmer's job is to grow food or raise animals for others to buy. Some farmers plant many acres, or fields, with different fruits, vegetables, or grains. Other farmers raise animals that are used for food or material. Cows can be used for meat, leather, and dairy products like milk and cheese. Chickens are raised for meat, eggs, and feathers. Pigs give us meat and leather. Sheep are used for their meat and wool. Each farmer helps feed the community or provides the animals to make the products we buy.

1. **What is the main idea of this story?**
    a. Farmers provide food and materials for products.
    b. Farmers raise cows.
    c. Meat, leather, and dairy products come from cows.
2. **Why don't most people grow their own food?**

_____

3. **What products do we get from cows?**

_____

4. **A word that means "large fields" is:**
    a. acres
    b. farm
    c. dairy products
5. **From which animal do we get wool?**

_____

6. **How do farmers help the community?**

_____

Think about it: Name three farm products your family uses.

Grocer

Most people in communities do not have time to go to farms to get their food. They buy food in places called grocery stores. The owner of a grocery store is called a grocer. He buys fresh fruit and vegetables from farmers. He buys canned and boxed foods from food packaging factories. Then he puts the food on shelves in his store and sells it to our families. The grocer offers many foods that we could not grow ourselves. He saves us time by gathering together different foods so we can go to one place to buy what we need.

1. **What is the main idea of this story?**
     a. Grocers buy food from farmers.
     b. People do not have time to go to farms.
     c. Grocers help us by gathering food in one place.
2. **Where do vegetables and fruits come from?**

_____

3. **Where do canned goods come from?**

_____

4. **What is a word that means "grocery store owner"?**
     a. grocer
     b. farm
     c. packaging factory
5. **What happens to food at a packaging factory?**

_____

6. **Why is a grocer so important to a community?**

_____

Think about it: Tell what things your family often gets at a grocery store.

Neighbors

The people that live near us are called neighbors. If you live in an apartment, the people in your building are your neighbors. If you live in a house, the people on your block are your neighbors. You see your neighbors during the day as they come and go or work in their yards. Neighbors know your name and help you in many ways. When you go on vacation a neighbor might pick up your mail or newspaper for you. They keep watch on your home to see that no one bothers it while you are away. Neighbors often borrow things from each other. The people in the neighborhood help protect each other.

1. **What is the main idea of this story?**
   a. Neighbors help each other.
   b. Neighbors borrow things.
   c. A neighborhood is nice.

2. **Tell three ways neighbors help each other:**

   _____

   _____

3. **If you live in a house, who are your neighbors?**

   _____

4. **Where might you see your neighbor?**

   _____

5. **Why are neighbors important to a community?**

   _____

Think about it: Name two of your neighbors.

Restaurant

A community has many different people that help us in some way. It also has many businesses where we can buy goods. One business you can find in every community is a restaurant. A restaurant is a store that sells food that is ready to eat. Some restaurants sell fast food, or meals that you can get very quickly. They usually have a drive-through window so you can pick up food without getting out of your car. Other restaurants are dine in. You go inside these restaurants, sit at a table, and get waited on. You order from a menu, a list of food, and it is cooked while you wait. The people that take your order and bring the food are called waiters or waitresses. A restaurant helps us by serving food when we don't have time to cook for ourselves.

1. **What is the main idea of this story?**
   a. Waiters bring you food.
   b. A restaurant helps people who are too busy to cook.
   c. Fast food tastes good.
2. **What is a restaurant?**

   _____

3. **What is "fast food"?**

   _____

4. **A restaurant that serves food at a table is called:**
   a. fast food
   b. waiter
   c. dine in
5. **Waiter and waitress are names of people who:**
   a. serve you food
   b. own restaurants
   c. sell food

Think about it: What is the name of your favorite restaurant?

School

One very important part of every community is a school. A school is a place where people become educated about the world. There are a few different kinds of schools. Elementary, junior high, and high schools are places where children go to learn math, reading, history, and science. After high school, some people go to trade school where they can learn skills for becoming a secretary or truck driver. Other people choose to go to college. College takes at least four years and prepares you for professional jobs like doctor, lawyer, or scientist. Without schools it would be hard to learn what we need to know to get a good job.

1. **What is the main idea of this story?**
   a. Schools teach us about the world.
   b. Trade schools teach skills.
   c. You can't get a job without school.
2. **What three types of schools educate children?**

_____

3. **What school teaches job skills?**

_____

4. **What school prepares you for a profession?**

_____

5. **What does educate mean?**
   a. school
   b. professional
   c. learn
6. **Why are schools important to a community?**

_____

Think about it: What job would you like? What school will help you prepare for this job?

Library

    A library is a place where you can borrow books to read. The library has many different kinds of books. There are fiction books to read for fun. There are how-to books that explain how to do things like fix a bike or make a model rocket. Reference books are full of facts we might want to know more about. A person called a librarian keeps the books in order and helps us find what we are looking for. We can borrow books for a week or two, but we must return them so others can use them, too. You need a library card in order to borrow books. The librarian can help you get one.

1. What is the main idea of this story?
    a. You can find many books in a library.
    b. Librarians help you find books.
    c. You need a library card.

2. What is a library?

_____

3. Name three kinds of books you can find in a library.

_____

4. Why must you return the books?

_____

5. The person who works in the library is a:
    a. teacher
    b. book
    c. librarian

6. Why are libraries important to a community?

_____

_____

Think about it: What is the name of your school librarian?

Hospital

Every large community has a hospital. A hospital is a place where people go when they are very sick or hurt. Doctors and nurses work there. If your tonsils hurt, you might go to a hospital to have them taken out. The doctor will put you to sleep then take you to the operating room. This is a very clean room where doctors remove or fix things inside your body. When someone gets hurt in an accident, they are taken to a hospital where they can be helped. Most hospitals also have a nursery. That is the place where babies are kept for the first few days after birth. The hospital nursery takes care of new babies and makes sure that they are healthy. Hospitals do a good job of helping the community stay healthy!

1. **What is the main idea of this story?**
   a. A hospital is a very clean place.
   b. Hospitals help very sick or hurt people.
   c. Hospitals have a nursery for babies.
2. **Who works in a hospital?**

_____

3. **When might someone go to a hospital?**

_____

4. **What is an operating room?**

_____

5. **What is a room for babies?**
   a. operating room
   b. nursery
   c. hospital
6. **How are hospitals important to a community?**

_____

Think about it: Tell about a time when you were in or visited a hospital.

Department Store

A department store is a large place that sells many different goods. A department is a group or area of things that are alike. There are clothes, tool, toy, garden, shoe, and kitchen departments all in the same store. If you need a pair of shoes and a hammer you do not need to go to a clothes store and a hardware store. You can get both things in one stop at a department store. This kind of shopping takes less time and is easy or convenient for most people.

1. **What is the main idea of this story?**
   a. Department stores make shopping easier.
   b. Shoes and hammers are sold together.
   c. A store is convenient.
2. **What is a department store?**

_____

3. **What is another name for an area where things are alike?**
   a. same
   b. store
   c. department
4. **What word in the story means easy?**
   a. convenient
   b. shopping
   c. department
5. **What departments might you find in a department store?**

_____

_____

6. **How does a department store help a community?**

_____

Think about it: Name a department store you have been to.

Gas Station

An important business for any community is a gas station. This is a place where we can get gasoline for our cars and trucks. A gas station can also fix your vehicle if it is not working right. They have pumps to put air in bicycle or car tires. They sell maps of the city or state to help you on the road. Some gas stations even have a car wash to keep your vehicle clean! This business is important because we use our cars or trucks every day. If your car is broken or out of gas you cannot go very far from home.

1. **What is the main idea of this story?**
   a. Gas stations sell gasoline.
   b. A gas station helps keep our vehicles running.
   c. We can buy maps at a gas station.

2. **What is a gas station?**

   _____

3. **Name four things you can get or do at a gas station:**

   _____

   _____

   _____

   _____

4. **What is another word for cars and trucks?**
   a. pumps
   b. vehicles
   c. bicycles

5. **Why are gas stations important to a community?**

   _____

Think about it: Draw a picture of the gas station you go to.

Park

Every community usually has a park for people to use. A park is an area set aside for recreation, or fun activities. There is a playground for children. It has swings, slides, or monkey bars to play on. Many parks have football fields, baseball diamonds, soccer fields, and a track for running. You can find picnic tables to sit on while you eat your lunch or dinner. Many parks have trees and a pond or lake to enjoy. A park is where people of the community can relax and have fun when they are not at school or work.

1. What is the main idea of this story?
   a. Parks are places were people relax.
   b. You can eat your lunch at a table.
   c. People don't like to work.

2. What is a park?

_____

3. Name three things you might do at a park:

_____

_____

_____

4. What is another word for fun activities?
   a. parks
   b. relax
   c. recreation

5. How are parks important to a community?

_____

Think about it: Draw a picture of yourself at a park.

Read the story.

Craig and Ernie

Mother gives Craig and his friend Ernie some chocolate cake. Craig thinks chocolate cake is the best kind of cake. Ernie likes chocolate cake, but thinks that yellow cake is even better. They eat all of the cake. Now they are thirsty and want some milk. They both agree that white milk is better than chocolate milk!

Tell whether each sentence is a fact (F) or an opinion (O):

_____Mother gave Craig and Ernie some chocolate cake.

_____Chocolate cake is the best kind of cake.

_____Ernie likes yellow cake better than chocolate cake.

_____Yellow cake is better than chocolate cake.

_____Craig and Ernie drank a glass of white milk.

_____White milk is better than chocolate milk.

Write one fact about this story.

_____

_____

Write one opinion about this story.

_____

_____

Read the story.

Vinnie

Vinnie loves children. He tells good jokes and makes up great stories for them. Children like Vinnie, too. They think he tells the best stories they have ever heard. They like to laugh at his silly jokes. Once Vinnie told a joke and then laughed so hard he fell off his chair. The children thought that was very funny. Vinnie didn't!

Tell whether each sentence is a fact (F) or an opinion (O):

_____Vinnie loves children.

_____Vinnie tells jokes and stories.

_____Children like Vinnie.

_____He tells stories better than anyone else.

_____Vinnie fell off his chair.

_____His fall was very funny.

Write one fact about this story.

_____

_____

Write one opinion about this story.

_____

_____

Read the story.

Which is Better?

The teacher let us draw pictures today. I drew a big blue flower. Patty drew a lot of little yellow flowers. Val drew three purple birds. The teacher said that all three drawings were very nice. Patty thinks that her picture is really prettier than mine. Val says that hers is the nicest. I am sure that mine is really the best of all.

Tell whether each sentence is a fact (F) or an opinion (O):

_____Patty drew the prettier flowers.

_____I drew the prettier flowers.

_____Val drew three purple birds.

_____The teacher said they were all very nice.

_____Blue is prettier than yellow.

_____All the pictures are the wrong color.

Write one fact about this story.

_____

_____

Write one opinion about this story.

_____

_____

Read the story.

Swimming

Swimming in my pool is better than swimming in a lake! My pool is in my back yard. I have to have Mom or Dad drive me to the lake. My pool is not as deep as the lake. I have some steps to sit on in my pool. The lake has a sandy beach to sit on. I do not like sand in my swimsuit. I am happy that I have such a nice pool. It is much better than any lake.

Tell whether each sentence is a fact (F) or an opinion (O):

_____A pool is better than a lake.

_____My pool is at my house.

_____The lake is too deep.

_____I can sit on the steps in my pool.

_____The sand is not very nice to sit on.

_____My pool makes me happy.

Write one fact about this story.

_____

_____

Write one opinion about this story.

_____

_____

Read the story.

Fall Leaves

Fall is the best season of all. In the summer all the leaves are green. In the winter there are no leaves at all. In the fall the leaves turn orange, yellow, red, and brown. Later, when the leaves fall from the trees, we can rake them into big piles. I love to make one large pile and then jump into it. It is so much fun to land on a soft pile of leaves.

Tell whether each sentence is a fact (F) or an opinion (O):

_____Fall is better than summer or winter.

_____In fall the leaves turn colors.

_____Leaves fall from the trees in the fall season.

_____We can rake the leaves into big piles.

_____Raking leaves is a lot of fun.

_____Leaves are pretty when they change colors.

Write one fact about this story.

_____

_____

Write one opinion about this story.

_____

_____

Using the first two letters in each word below, write each word in the correct column.

blue	sleep	clock	slow
clue	slap	black	blend
slip	climb	blind	clown
clan	blank	slope	bleed
clean	slab	class	slipper
block	slam	cloud	bloom

bl   **sl**   **cl**

_____   _____   _____

_____   _____   _____

_____   _____   _____

_____   _____   _____

_____   _____   _____

_____   _____   _____

_____   _____   _____

THINK AHEAD: Can you find another bl, sl, and cl word?

bl _____   sl _____   cl _____

Using the first two letters from each word below, write each word in the correct column.

ship	slump	shot	slur
star	shut	stamp	stump
slim	shoot	stem	stir
shall	slap	sled	slit
shoe	stain	sheep	slat
shack	stall	sling	sting

st   **sh**   **sl**

_____   _____   _____

_____   _____   _____

_____   _____   _____

_____   _____   _____

_____   _____   _____

_____   _____   _____

_____   _____   _____

THINK AHEAD: Can you find another st, sh, and sl word?

st _____   sh _____   sl _____

Using the first two letters in each word below, write each word in the correct column.

crow	true	from	crown
frock	trick	frog	trash
crumb	tree	fruit	cram
trunk	cream	critter	frame
train	track	freeze	crook
trace	crew	friend	free

tr   **fr**   **cr**

_____   _____   _____

_____   _____   _____

_____   _____   _____

_____   _____   _____

_____   _____   _____

_____   _____   _____

_____   _____   _____

THINK AHEAD: Can you find another tr, fr, and cr word?

tr _____   fr _____   cr _____

Use the words in the list below to make three groups of words. Write the words that end in "ck" or "sh" in the first two columns. Find the third group by looking at the last two letters of the remaining words. Label the third column with these two letters. Write the words in this column.

fish	tack	nick	flash
first	fast	wash	last
trick	chick	list	wish
check	trash	nest	mash
east	chuck	truck	mush
dish	west	track	cast

ck   **sh**   _____

_____   _____   _____

_____   _____   _____

_____   _____   _____

_____   _____   _____

_____   _____   _____

_____   _____   _____

_____   _____   _____

THINK AHEAD: Can you find another ck, sh, and _____ word?

tr _____   fr _____   ___ _____

Name _____   skill: blends

Use the words in the list below to make three groups of words. Write the words that begin with "str" or "squ" in the first two columns. Find the third group by looking at the first three letters of the remaining words. Label the third column with these three letters. Write the words in this column.

straw	squash	scream	squish
string	scram	strum	scrap
squirrel	strap	squiggle	scrape
scroll	squid	script	stripe
squall	strand	stream	scramble
squander	scribble	squabble	strut

str   **squ**   _____

_____   _____   _____

_____   _____   _____

_____   _____   _____

_____   _____   _____

_____   _____   _____

_____   _____   _____

_____   _____   _____

THINK AHEAD: Can you find another str, squ , and _____ word

str_____   squ _____   ___ _____

Use the words in the list below to make three groups of words. Write the words that begin with "ch" or "sh" in the first two columns. Find the third group by looking at the first two letters of the remaining words. Label the third column with these two letters and write the words in the column.

thin	shine	chair	share
think	choose	chin	should
thank	thunder	chain	shiny
cheese	child	shut	thimble
thistle	shell	shed	chat
thug	thigh	shoot	cheer

ch   **sh**   _____

_____   _____   _____

_____   _____   _____

_____   _____   _____

_____   _____   _____

_____   _____   _____

_____   _____   _____

_____   _____   _____

THINK AHEAD: Can you find another ch, sh , and ____ word?

ch _____   sh _____   ___ _____

Name _____   skill: blends

Use the words in the list below to make three groups of words. Write the
words that begin with "dr" in the first column. Label the remaining two
columns by looking at the first two letters of the leftover words. Write the
words in the correct columns.

price	draw	prom	tree
prod	droop	trim	trance
troop	dream	proof	drip
prune	prime	drop	track
treat	prank	drape	dram
trick	drool	trot	prim

dr   _____   _____

_____   _____   _____

_____   _____   _____

_____   _____   _____

_____   _____   _____

_____   _____   _____

_____   _____   _____

_____   _____   _____

THINK AHEAD: Can you find another dr, _____ , and _____ word?

dr _____   ___ _____   ___ _____

Name _____   skill: blends

Use the words in the list below to make three groups of words. Write the words that begin with "br" in the first column. Label the remaining two columns by looking at the first two letters of the leftover words. Write the words in the correct columns.

bright	green	brick	from
froth	grit	brought	bring
gross	frog	fry	grab
grope	broke	frail	freak
grew	grow	branch	frost
brunch	grunt	brat	frank

br _____   _____

_____   _____   _____

_____   _____   _____

_____   _____   _____

_____   _____   _____

_____   _____   _____

_____   _____   _____

_____   _____   _____

THINK AHEAD: Can you find another br, _____ , and _____ word?

br _____   ___ _____   ___ _____

Name _____   skill: blends

Use the words in the list below to make three groups of words. Write the words that end in "ch" in the first column. Label the remaining two columns by looking at the last two letters of the leftover words. Write the words in the correct columns.

dent	bent	blind	bind
which	bend	inch	itch
blend	bunt	vent	latch
switch	brand	meant	lint
sand	bench	pond	lunch
land	mint	bunch	mount

ch   _____   _____

_____   _____   _____

_____   _____   _____

_____   _____   _____

_____   _____   _____

_____   _____   _____

_____   _____   _____

_____   _____   _____

THINK AHEAD: Can you find another ch, _____ , and _____ word?

ch _____   ___ _____   ___ _____

Use the words in the list below to make three groups of words. Label the three columns by looking at the first letters of each word. Write the words in the correct columns.

glass   flop   glow   stream
strand   glum   flower   gloomy
flank   strong   flunk   stroll
streak   glad   flip   glint
strum   flour   glue   flap
strive   fleece   glove   struck

_____   _____   _____

_____   _____   _____

_____   _____   _____

_____   _____   _____

_____   _____   _____

_____   _____   _____

_____   _____   _____

THINK AHEAD: Can you find another word for each group?

_____   _____   _____

Name _____

Use the words in the list below to make three groups of words. Label the three columns by looking at the last two letters of each word. Write the words in the correct columns.

fist	host	pink	plank
struck	stack	tank	back
toast	sank	buck	mast
stuck	sunk	rust	dunk
must	tack	ink	first
cluck	clock	sink	dust

_____   _____   _____

_____   _____   _____

_____   _____   _____

_____   _____   _____

_____   _____   _____

_____   _____   _____

_____   _____   _____

THINK AHEAD: Can you find another word for each group?

_____   _____   _____

Name _____ skill: r controlled vowels

Use the words in the list below to make three groups of words. Write the words with "ar" or "ir", or "ur" in the correct columns.

card	bird	burn	first
turn	harp	girl	far
nurse	sir	purse	star
arm	shirt	skirt	spark
hurt	barn	curb	curve
birth	curtain	circle	market

ar   **ir**   **ur**

_____   _____   _____

_____   _____   _____

_____   _____   _____

_____   _____   _____

_____   _____   _____

_____   _____   _____

_____   _____   _____

THINK AHEAD: Can you find another word for each group?

_____   _____   _____

Name _____ skill: r controlled vowels

Use the words in the list below to make three groups of words. Write the words with "or" or "er" in the first two columns. Label the third column by looking at the letters of the remaining words. Write these words in the column.

garden	over	dart	corn
paper	word	diver	part
term	large	color	herd
horn	bar	pork	fern
morning	perch	tarp	torn
tar	tart	germ	cord

or   **er**   _____

_____   _____   _____

_____   _____   _____

_____   _____   _____

_____   _____   _____

_____   _____   _____

_____   _____   _____

_____   _____   _____

THINK AHEAD: Can you find another word for each group?

_____   _____   _____

Name _____ skill: r controlled vowels

Use the words in the list below to make three groups of words. Write the words with "ur" in the first column. Label the remaining columns by looking at the leftover words. Write the words in the correct columns.

curl	yarn	fur	cork
fork	harm	form	bark
lurk	march	purr	fort
spur	motor	start	odor
murky	orange	cart	jar
burr	organ	curd	sugar

ur _____ _____

_____ _____ _____

_____ _____ _____

_____ _____ _____

_____ _____ _____

_____ _____ _____

_____ _____ _____

_____ _____ _____

THINK AHEAD: Can you find another word for each group?

ur _____ _____

Use the words in the list below to make three groups of words. Each group should have the same vowel sound.   Write the words in the correct columns.

bike	side	beet	save
beam	tame	hate	bean
time	neat	line	mane
base	seem	name	fine
team	mice	nine	male
meat	case	hive	lean

long a	**long e**	**long i**
_____	_____	_____
_____	_____	_____
_____	_____	_____
_____	_____	_____
_____	_____	_____
_____	_____	_____
_____	_____	_____

THINK AHEAD: Can you find another word for each group?

_____   _____   _____

Name _____ skill: long vowels

Use the words in the list below to make three groups of words. Each group should have the same vowel sound. Write the words in the correct columns.

tube	shave	ruby	nose
tale	tone	mate	tune
bone	lane	cute	cone
mute	lone	lame	duty
fate	note	rule	globe
wage	June	wave	boat

long o   **long u**   **long a**

_____   _____   _____

_____   _____   _____

_____   _____   _____

_____   _____   _____

_____   _____   _____

_____   _____   _____

_____   _____   _____

THINK AHEAD: Can you find another word for each group?

_____   _____   _____

©1995 Kelley Wingate Publications, Inc.   90   CD-3709

Use the words in the list below to make three groups of words. Each group should have the same vowel sound. Write the words in the correct columns.

jam	ill	fed	tell
tan	sit	fill	ten
jack	get	van	fish
send	will	end	land
sat	bill	pal	vent
pin	neck	sad	

short a   **short e**   **short i**

_____   _____   _____

_____   _____   _____

_____   _____   _____

_____   _____   _____

_____   _____   _____

_____   _____   _____

THINK AHEAD: Can you find another word for each group?

_____   _____   _____

Use the words in the list below to make three groups of words. Each group should have the same vowel sound. Write the words in the correct columns.

odd	add	but	lap
cup	bad	cot	fun
dot	pond	sun	tap
not	cut	lot	and
jug	last	dog	fuss
man	pat	buff	log

short o   **short u**   **short a**

_____   _____   _____

_____   _____   _____

_____   _____   _____

_____   _____   _____

_____   _____   _____

_____   _____   _____

_____   _____   _____

THINK AHEAD: Can you find another word for each group?

_____   _____   _____

Name _____ skill: long and short vowels

Use the words in the list below to make two groups of words. Each group
should have words with either long vowel sounds or short vowel sounds.
Write the words in the correct columns.

teach	pint	take	glad
can	cent	see	sum
pal	poke	wind	fire
beat	true	tall	home
son	nut	hole	ate
new	bed	made	hat

Long Vowel Words   **Short Vowel Words**

_____ _____   _____ _____

_____ _____   _____ _____

_____ _____   _____ _____

_____ _____   _____ _____

_____ _____   _____ _____

_____ _____   _____ _____

THINK AHEAD: Can you find another word for each group?

_____ _____

Name _____   skill: long and short vowels

Use the words in the list below to make two groups of words. Each group should have words with either long vowel sounds or short vowel sounds. Write the words in the correct columns.

woke	date	use	shut
twin	wig	pile	nose
rug	bake	duck	mate
drag	fell	kick	kite
dive	hid	cone	coat
mop	tape	pin	nap

Long Vowel Words   **Short Vowel Words**

_____ _____   _____ _____

_____ _____   _____ _____

_____ _____   _____ _____

_____ _____   _____ _____

_____ _____   _____ _____

_____ _____   _____ _____

THINK AHEAD: Can you find another word for each group?

_____   _____

Read the story below. Rewrite the story by replacing each underlined word with a word from the list that means about the same thing.

Anita's Party

Anita is <u>having</u> a party. We <u>should</u> take a <u>present</u>. We will <u>put on</u> some <u>pretty</u> hats and play games. <u>After</u> we eat the cake it will be time to <u>go home</u>.

beautiful   following   gift   giving
leave   must   wear

_____

_____

_____

_____

_____

Draw a picture of the story.

Read the story below. Rewrite the story by replacing each underlined word with a word from the list that means about the same thing.

Toby

Toby is a <u>puppy</u>. He is <u>about</u> as <u>big</u> as a shoe box. He does not run <u>fast</u>. He is <u>slow</u>. He does not like to play with <u>very many</u> people. Toby is never <u>bad</u>. He does not <u>bite</u>. He <u>just</u> wants to be by himself!

around	dog	large
lots of	naughty	nip
only	pokey	quickly

_____

_____

_____

_____

_____

Draw a picture of the story.

Read the story below. Rewrite the story by replacing each underlined word with a word from the list that means about the same thing.

A Hot Day

Today is <u>hot</u>. We had a <u>drink</u> of <u>cold</u> water. We cannot <u>take a walk</u> or <u>throw</u> a ball. We wear <u>hats</u> to make <u>a shadow</u> on our faces. Too much sun can make anyone <u>sick</u>. It is best to stay <u>quiet</u> on a day like this.

caps	cool	hike
ill	shade	sip
still	toss	warm

_____

_____

_____

_____

_____

_____

Draw a picture of the story.

Read the story below. Rewrite the story by replacing each underlined word with a word from the list that means about the same thing.

Peter and I

Peter is a six year old <u>boy</u>. His <u>house</u> is <u>close</u> to mine. We are good <u>friends</u>. Today we got <u>wet</u> with the hose. I <u>smiled</u> when he got my <u>belly</u> wet. We both <u>laughed</u> when the water <u>splashed</u> my mom!

giggled	grinned	home
lad	near	pals
soaked	squirted	stomach

_____

_____

_____

_____

_____

_____

Draw a picture of the story.

Read the story below. Rewrite the story by replacing each underlined word with a word from the list that means about the same thing.

Mud

<u>Few</u> things are as <u>much fun</u> as getting <u>dirty</u>. First, <u>pick</u> a <u>large</u> <u>black</u> puddle to play in.   Next, <u>walk</u> in. It is great to <u>touch</u> the mud <u>around</u> your toes. It feels <u>good</u>! When you are <u>done</u> you must <u>wash</u> up.

between	big	choose	clean	dark
enjoyable	feel	finished	muddy	not many
wade	wonderful			

_____

_____

_____

_____

_____

Draw a picture of the story.

Name _____

Read the story below. Rewrite the story by replacing each underlined word with a word from the list that means about the same thing.

A Bad Day

It was not a good day. I got up at sunrise and was tired all day. Mom forgot to iron my shirt. I ripped my pants. I lost my best two socks. I hit my arm as I hurried to school. I will be happy when this day is over!

arose	banged	dawn	glad
finished	nice	pair of	press
rushed	sleepy	tore	trousers

_____

_____

_____

_____

_____

_____

Draw a picture of the story.

Read the story below. Rewrite the story by replacing each underlined word with a word from the list that means about the same thing.

The Yellow Taxi

The yellow <u>taxi</u> <u>rushed</u> <u>bravely</u> down the <u>busy</u> street. Its yellow paint was <u>shining</u> brightly in the evening sun. The cab <u>had</u> to <u>get to</u> the other side of the <u>city</u> before <u>sundown</u>. The ride <u>was over</u> as they <u>came to</u> the train station. That was not so <u>hard</u>!

arrived at	cab	crowded	difficult	dusk
ended	fearlessly	glowing	needed	reach
sped	town			

_____

_____

_____

_____

_____

_____

Draw a picture of the story.

Read the story below. Rewrite the story by replacing each underlined word with a word from the list that means the opposite.

Jody

Jody was <u>working</u> hard.
<u>She</u> was <u>pulling</u> <u>her</u> blocks <u>together</u>.
<u>She</u> put <u>a few</u> <u>on top of</u> the chair.
Jody built a <u>big</u> wall without using all of <u>her</u> blocks!

apart	he	he	little	many
his	playing	pushing	under	his

_____

_____

_____

_____

_____

Draw a picture of the story.

Read the story below. Rewrite the story by replacing each underlined word with a word from the list that means the opposite.

A New Pet
The little girl has a new pet.
It is a black dog with soft fur.
The girl has many pets that run fast.
She likes to play with them.

an	old	slow	boy	few	he
slowly	walk	white	boy	hard	

_____

_____

_____

_____

_____

Draw a picture of the story.

Read the story below. Rewrite the story by replacing each underlined word with a word from the list that means the opposite.

A Cold Drink

It was a <u>hot</u> <u>day</u>.
The <u>boy</u> was <u>standing</u> under a tree.
<u>He</u> wanted a <u>cold</u> drink of tea.
The <u>sun</u> began to <u>sink</u> in the sky.
<u>He</u> <u>quickly</u> <u>cooled</u> <u>down</u>.

cold	girl	hot	moon	night	rise	she
she	sitting	slowly	up	warmed		

_____

_____

_____

_____

_____

Draw a picture of the story.

Read the story below. Rewrite the story by replacing each underlined word with a word from the list that means the opposite.

Jack

Jack the puppy has <u>a hard</u> job.
He must <u>learn</u> <u>many</u> things each <u>day</u>.
He must <u>walk</u> and <u>stay</u> when told.
He works with the same <u>boy</u> every <u>morning</u>.
The <u>hardest</u> job of all is to be <u>quiet</u> when he sees a cat.

an easy	easiest	evening	a few	girl
go	night	noisy	plays	run
teach				

_____

_____

_____

_____

_____

Draw a picture of the story.

©1995 Kelley Wingate Publications, Inc.   CD-3709

Read the story below. Rewrite the story by replacing each underlined word with a word from the list that means the opposite.

A Bad Day
Today was a <u>bad</u> day.
I <u>lost</u> my <u>left</u> shoe.
I was <u>late</u> for class and <u>last</u> in line.
I got all of my work <u>wrong</u>.
I almost <u>cried</u> because I was so <u>sad</u>.
<u>Tomorrow</u> <u>will be</u> a <u>better</u> day!

correct	early	first	found
good	happy	laughed	right
was	worse	yesterday	

_____

_____

_____

_____

_____

Draw a picture of the story.

Read the story below. Rewrite the story by replacing each underlined word with a word from the list that means the opposite.

Al and the Cat
Al was <u>brave</u> today.
<u>He</u> found a <u>thin</u>, <u>wild</u> cat that was <u>hungry</u>.
The cat <u>opened</u> its mouth.
Al put <u>his</u> hand <u>over</u> the cat's face.
The cat licked Al with its <u>warm</u>, <u>rough</u> tongue.

closed	cool	fat	full
her	scared	she	smooth
tame	under		

_____

_____

_____

_____

_____

_____

Draw a picture of the story.

Name _____   skill: antonyms

Read the story below. Rewrite the story by replacing each underlined word
with a word from the list that means the opposite.

Sal

There was once a <u>strong</u> <u>man</u> named Sal.
<u>He</u> was <u>large</u> and very <u>tall</u>.
Sal could lift <u>many</u> <u>heavy</u> things <u>above</u> <u>his</u> shoulders.
On <u>winter</u> <u>mornings</u> at <u>sunrise</u> <u>he</u> liked to take long walks.
Sal would leave the house <u>before</u> it got <u>light</u> outside.

after	dark	evenings	few
light	she	short	summer
sunset	tiny	below	weak
woman	her	She	

_____

_____

_____

_____

_____

Draw a picture of the story.

Answer Key

Name _____   skill: sequencing

1. Read the story

Kelly

Kelly takes off her shoes. She puts on her roller skates. Pull the laces tight, Kelly. You must tie them so the laces are not too long. Kelly stands up. She takes two tiny steps. Watch out!

2. Read the sentences below. Write them in order as they happened in the story.

1. Kelly's shoes come off.
2. She puts on roller skates.
3. Kelly makes sure the laces are tight.
4. She stands up.
5. Kelly steps two times.

She puts on roller skates.
Kelly's shoes come off.
She stands up.
Kelly makes sure the laces are tight.
Kelly steps two times.

3. Draw a line under the best ending for this story.
Kelly takes off the skates.
<u>Kelly falls down.</u>
The roller skates need new laces.

©1995 Kelley Wingate Publications, Inc.   5   KW 1012

Name _____   skill: sequencing

1. Read the story.

Growing Flowers

Growing potted flowers is fun. Fill a pot with dirt. Plant seeds. Water them everyday. Soon the stems and leaves will grow. Pull any weeds that come up. Buds will pop out in a few weeks.

2. Read the sentences below. Write them in order as they happened in the story.

Water the seeds.
Buds grow on the stems.
Put dirt in a pot.
Pull the weeds.
Plant the flower seeds.

1. Put dirt in a pot.
2. Plant the flower seeds.
3. Water the seeds.
4. Pull the weeds.
5. Buds grow on the stem.

3. Draw a line under the best ending for this story.
Give the pot away.
Put the pot outside in the sun.
<u>Flowers will bloom.</u>

©1995 Kelley Wingate Publications, Inc.   6   KW 1012

Name _____   skill: sequencing

1. Read the story.

Fridays

Friday is the best day of all. Mom picks me up from school. Then, we get an ice cream cone. I like chocolate the best. We go to the park then have pizza for dinner. Sometimes we go to a movie.

2. Read the sentences below. Write them in order as they happened in the story.

1. Fridays are good days.
2. I have chocolate ice cream.
3. We play at the park.
4. We have pizza for dinner.
5. We go to a movie.

We have pizza for dinner.
I have chocolate ice cream.
We go to a movie.
Fridays are good days.
We play at the park.

3. Draw a line under the best ending for this story.
<u>I am tired and go right to bed.</u>
I do my homework.
Mom takes me back to school.

©1995 Kelley Wingate Publications, Inc.   7   KW 1012

Name _____   skill: sequencing

1. Read the story.

Meyer and Tim

Meyer is a little boy. He has a puppy named Tim. Tim is also very young. Meyer and Tim are good friends. They play ball together. They take naps together. After their nap they share a snack.

2. Read the sentences below. Write them in order as they happened in the story.

1. Meyer and Tim are both young.
2. They are good friends.
3. They play ball together.
4. They slept at the same time.
5. Meyer and Tim ate a snack.

They are good friends.
They slept at the same time.
Meyer and Tim are both young.
They play ball together.
Meyer and Tim ate a snack.

3. Draw a line under the best ending for this story.
Meyer plays with another boy.
Tim eats a bone.
<u>Tim sleeps all night on Meyer's bed.</u>

©1995 Kelley Wingate Publications, Inc.   8   KW 1012

Answer Key

Name _____ skill: sequencing
1. Read the story.

Crossing the Street
It is important to be safe. Crossing a street the right way will help keep you safe. Walk to the corner. Stop at the curb. Look left and right. When there are no cars coming, it is safe to cross.

2. Read the sentences below. Write them in order as they happened in the story.

1. Crossing streets safely is important.
2. Go to the corner.
3. Stop at the corner.
4. Look both ways for cars.
5. Cross when it is safe.

Cross when it is safe.
Look both ways for cars.
Crossing streets safely is important.
Stop at the corner.
Go to the corner.

3. Draw a line under the best ending for this story.
Wait for cars to come.
Look once more then walk across the street.
Quickly run across the street.

©1995 Kelley Wingate Publications, Inc.   9   KW 1012

Name _____ skill: sequencing
1. Read the story.

Mike
Mike loves to swing. He comes to the playground. It takes time to find the right swing. Mike sits down and pushes with his feet. He leans forward and backward. Look how high he goes!

2. Read the sentences below. Write them in order as they happened in the story.

1. Mike goes to the playground.
2. He finds a swing that is just right.
3. Mike pushes with his feet.
4. He swings back and forth to make the swing go.
5. Mike swings very high.

Mike pushes with his feet.
Mike swings very high.
He leans back and forth to make the swing go.
Mike goes to the playground.
He finds a swing that is just right.

3. Draw a line under the best ending for this story.
Mike swings until he is tired.
Mother calls Mike home.
He stops swinging and plays on the slide.

©1995 Kelley Wingate Publications, Inc.   10   KW 1012

Name _____ skill: sequencing
1. Read the story.

Elly and the Cookie
Mother baked cookies. She gave one to Elly. Oh, it smelled good! Elly took the cookie outside. She sat down to eat it. A little squirrel came up to Elly's foot. It looked hungry. Elly gave the squirrel a piece of cookie. Oh, it tasted good!

2. Read the sentences below. Write them in order as they happened in the story.

1. The cookie smelled good.
2. She went outside to eat the cookie.
3. A squirrel came close to Elly.
4. The squirrel looked hungry.
5. She gave some cookie to the squirrel.

She went outside to eat the cookie.
The cookie smelled good.
A squirrel came close to Elly.
She gave some cookie to the squirrel.
The squirrel looked hungry.

3. Draw a line under the best ending for this story.
Elly got angry with the squirrel.
The squirrel called his friends.
They both enjoyed the rest of the cookie.

©1995 Kelley Wingate Publications, Inc.   11   KW 1012

Name _____ skill: sequencing
1. Read the story.

Alyssa's Dance
Alyssa loves to dance for Mother. First, Alyssa stands on her toes. Then, she spins in circles. After that, she hops and leaps. Alyssa swings her arms over her head and bends to one side. Last, she bows to her mother.

2. Read the sentences below. Write them in order as they happened in the story.

1. Dancing is fun for Alyssa.
2. She stands on tip-toe then spins around.
3. Hopping and leaping comes next.
4. She sways her arms back and forth.
5. Alyssa bows low for her mother.

Hopping and leaping comes next.
She sways her arms back and forth.
Alyssa bows low for her mother.
She stands on tip-toe then spins around.
Dancing is fun for Alyssa.

3. Draw a line under the best ending for this story.
Alyssa stands on her toes.
Alyssa goes to sleep
Mother claps and smiles.

©1995 Kelley Wingate Publications, Inc.   12   KW 1012

Answer Key

Name _____ skill: sequencing

1. Read the story.

Roger Rides His Bike

Roger can do tricks on his bike. In June he learned to ride very fast. In July he could ride while standing up. By August Roger could ride with no hands. I think he will ride without hands or feet soon! He learns very quickly.

2. Read the sentences in the box below. Write them in order as they happened in the story.

1. Roger does tricks.
2. He rides quickly.
3. He can stand and ride the bike.
4. He does not use his hands.
5. He might ride without using his hands.

He does not use his hands.
He might ride without using his feet.
Roger does tricks.
He rides quickly.
He can stand and ride the bike.

3. Draw a line under the best ending for this story.
<u>Roger becomes a great bike rider.</u>
Roger becomes a football player.
Roger sells his bike.

©1995 Kelley Wingate Publications, Inc.   13   KW 1012

Name _____ skill: sequencing

1. Read the story.

A Rock Collection

Collecting rocks is a fun hobby. First you must find some small rocks. Look for odd shapes or pretty colors. Wash away all the dirt. Put the rocks in a jar and cover them with water. Put a lid on the jar. The water makes the pretty colors brighter.

2. Read the sentences below. Write them in order as they happened in the story.

1. Rock collecting is a fun hobby
2. Find some pretty or odd shaped rocks.
3. Wash the rocks to get rid of the dirt.
4. Put the rocks into a jar.
5. Cover the rocks with water.

Put the rocks into a jar.
Rock collecting is a fun hobby.
Cover the rocks with water.
Wash the rocks to get rid of the dirt.
Find some pretty or odd shaped rocks.

3. Draw a line under the best ending for this story.
<u>Put the jar on a shelf so you can look at it.</u>
Throw the rocks away.
Start a button collection.

©1995 Kelley Wingate Publications, Inc.   14   KW 1012

Name _____ skill: comprehension

Tina is very tiny. She is the smallest girl in her class. Her desk is big. The chalkboard is too high. Tina is happy, though. She is very good at many things. She is a good reader. She is a great speller. When she plays hide and seek, no one can find Tina!

1. A good title for this story would be:
  a. Hide and Seek
  (b.) Tiny Tina
  c. A Good Speller

2. What two things are too big for Tina?

a. chalkboard

b. desk

3. Why is Tina happy about herself?

a. She is a good reader.

b. She is a good speller.

4. What can Tina do better than most people?

She plays hide and seek.

5. Tell something else that a small person might be better at than a big person.

answers will vary

©1995 Kelley Wingate Publications, Inc.   15   KW 1012

Name _____ skill: comprehension

Joey watched some children having a race. He wanted to join them, but he couldn't. Joey could not run. He could not walk. Joey had been in a wheelchair his whole life. The children saw Joey. They asked him if he would help them. They needed someone to decide who the winner of the race was. Joey was pleased. Everyone had a good time.

1. A good title for this story would be:
  a. The Race
  (b. How Joey Helped)
  c. A Wheelchair

2. What did Joey want to do?

He wanted to join in the race.

3. Why couldn't Joey be in the race?

He could not walk

4. How did the children get Joey to play?

They needed someone to decide the winner of the race.

5. How do you think Joey felt at the beginning of the story?

unhappy

©1995 Kelley Wingate Publications, Inc.   16   KW 1012

Answer Key

Name _____ skill: comprehension

Sunlight was shining from a silver sky. The weather was warming the woods. A baby bear was biting blueberries from a big bush. Bees buzzed in a bluebonnet bloom. Four frogs flicked fat flippers. Two turtles tucked in their tails. Spring season is special!

1. A good title for this story would be:
    a. Four Frogs in a Pond
    (b. A Sunny Spring Day)
    c. Baby Bear and the Blueberries

2. What was baby bear eating?

blueberries

3. Where were the bees?

in a bluebonnet bloom

4. What is different about the words in this story?

The words begin with the same consonant.

5. Write a sentence about Mary Mouse. Make most of the words begin with the letter "m".

answers will vary

Name _____ skill: comprehension

A treehouse is a wonderful place to play. If you hide behind the leaves, no one will see you. Sit very still and you might see squirrels or birds playing in the tree. In a treehouse you can read a good book. You can daydream about what you will be someday. You can even pretend to be a pirate or an explorer. Ask a friend to come into your treehouse and you can have even more fun!

1. A good title for this story would be:
    (a. A Treehouse)
    b. Hiding in the Leaves
    c. A Good Way to Watch Birds

2. What are two things you can pretend to be in a treehouse?

a pirate or explorer

3. Why do you need to sit still to watch birds and squirrels?

if you move you may scare them away

4. Why might you hide behind the leaves?

so that the animals will not see you.

5. What might you do with a friend in your treehouse?

answers will vary

Name _____ skill: comprehension

I have a new baby sister. Her name is Amanda. Mom and Dad brought her home from the hospital last week. I want to play games with her but Mom says she is too little. She sleeps a lot. She cries a lot. She sure can't do much! She does like to watch me when she is awake. I hope she gets bigger soon.

1. A good title for this story would be:
    a. Growing Up
    b. Babies
    (c. My Sister Amanda)

2. When did Amanda come home?

last week

3. What are two things that Amanda can do?

a. _sleep a lot_

b. _cry a lot_

4. Why do I want Amanda to get bigger soon?

so I can play games with her

5. What are two things you can do with a new baby?

a. _answers will vary_

b. _____

Name _____ skill: comprehension

I went shopping with Dad last week. We walked past many rows of toys. I stopped to look at one toy that I really wanted to buy. When I looked up, Dad was gone! I did not move, but looked as far as I could see down the aisle. Dad was not there. I knew he was lost! "Dad?" I called. He came from around the corner. Dad was not lost anymore.

1. A good title for this story would be:
    a. Shopping with Dad
    (b. Lost!)
    c. Finding a Toy

2. What did I stop to look at?

a toy

3. A word that means "row" or "pathway" is:
    a. corner
    b. store
    (c. aisle)

4. What did I do to try and find Dad?

a. _I looked down the aisle_

b. _I called, "Dad?"_

5. Was it really Dad or the child who was lost? Explain.

The child

Answer Key

Dorothy got a box of magic tricks for her birthday. She learned how to change one coin into another. She learned how to make two pieces of rope turn into one piece of rope. Dorothy put on a magic show for her friends. They liked her tricks very much. The magic box was Dorothy's favorite birthday present.

1. **A good title for this story would be:**
   a. Dorothy's Magic Box ⟵ (circled)
   b. The Best Birthday
   c. Dorothy Puts on a Show

2. **What could she do with two pieces of rope?**
   make it turn into one piece of rope

3. **How did Dorothy's friends feel about her show?**
   They liked it

4. **What is another word for "favorite"?**
   a. best loved ⟵ (circled)
   b. worst
   c. easy to use

5. **Which trick would you like to learn to do? Why?**
   answers will vary

©1995 Kelley Wingate Publications, Inc.   21   KW 1012

Chuck lives in the country. He has a big barn and a lot of land, but no animals. Chuck does not grow animals. He grows trees. Chuck has many kinds of fruit trees. He grows pear, apple, cherry, and plum trees. Each spring and fall he is busy picking their fruit. It is fun to go to Chuck's farm when the fruit is ripe. Yum, yum!

1. **A good title for this story would be:**
   a. Fruit Tastes Good
   b. Many Trees
   c. Chuck's Fruit Farm ⟵ (circled)

2. **Why doesn't Chuck have animals?**
   He does not grow animals

3. **What four kinds of fruit does Chuck grow?**
   pear, apple, cherry, plum

4. **The word "ripe" means:**
   a. growing
   b. ready to pick ⟵ (circled)
   c. red

5. **Name two other fruits that grow on trees.**
   a. answers will vary
   b. _____

©1995 Kelley Wingate Publications, Inc.   22   KW 1012

There is a new boy in our class. His name is Brian. Today is his first day at our school. He rode to school on my bus. He was very quiet at lunch. He stood near the wall and did not play during recess. I think he might be nice because he smiled whenever I looked at him. He might just be bashful. Do you think we could become friends?

1. **A good title for this story would be:**
   a. A New Boy ⟵ (circled)
   b. Brian is quiet
   c. My Friend

2. **What two things does Brian do that show me he is bashful?**
   a. he was very quiet at lunch
   b. he did not play during recess

3. **What makes me think Brian is nice?**
   he smiled at me when I looked at him

4. **What word means the same as "bashful"?**
   a. shy ⟵ (circled)
   b. loud
   c. unfriendly

5. **What can I do to become friends with the new boy?**
   answers will vary

©1995 Kelley Wingate Publications, Inc.   23   KW 1012

Joe is the man who lives next door. Mother says he is pretty old, but I don't think so. Joe is always in his yard when I come home from school. He invites me to sit on the front steps with him. He listens to me as I tell him about my day at school. He tells wonderful stories that make me laugh and laugh. Joe may be old in years, but he is my best friend!

1. **A good title for this story would be:**
   a. Joe Tells Stories
   b. An Old Man
   c. My Friend Joe ⟵ (circled)

2. **What does Mother think about Joe?**
   She thinks he is pretty old

3. **What two things make me like Joe so much?**
   a. He listens to me as I tell him about my day at school.
   b. He makes me laugh.

4. **Another word for "invite" is:**
   a. tell
   b. ask ⟵ (circled)
   c. pick

5. **What other things can older people and children enjoy together?**
   answers will vary

©1995 Kelley Wingate Publications, Inc.   24   KW 1012

Answer Key

Name _____ skill: comprehension

Parts of the Body

Your body has many parts. Some parts protect you, or keep you safe. Your skin covers your body. It protects the things inside you. Some body parts help you learn about things. They are called your senses. Your eyes let you see what is around you. You listen with your ears. You learn smells by using your nose. Your mouth lets you taste things. Skin helps you learn how things feel. All of these parts are on the outside of your body.

1. What is the main idea of this story?
   a. Your body has many parts.
   b. Skin protects other parts inside your body.
   c. We learn using our eyes.

2. Name five parts of your body.
   eyes, ears, nose, mouth, skin

3. The word protect means:
   a. feel
   b. skin
   c. keep safe

4. What does skin do?
   keeps you safe, helps you learn how things feel.

5. What outside body parts help you learn?
   eyes, ears, nose, mouth

6. How do body parts help you learn?
   They help you explore things around you.

©1995 Kelley Wingate Publications, Inc.   25   KW 1012

Name _____ skill: comprehension

Inside the Body

Many body parts cannot be seen because they are inside the body. Bones and muscles are inside your body. Some body parts are called organs. Organs are body parts that do special jobs. Your brain, heart, and lungs are organs. They do special jobs that help you. Your brain helps you think. Your heart pumps your blood. Your lungs help you breathe. You do not have to think about making them work. They do their jobs automatically, without you telling them.

1. What is the main idea of this story?
   a. Organs are parts inside your body that do special jobs.
   b. You do not have to tell organs to do their jobs.
   c. Some parts are inside the body.

2. The word "organ" means:
   a. to think about
   b. bones and muscles
   c. body parts that do special jobs

3. Name three organs.
   brain, heart, lungs

4. "Automatically" means:
   a. without thinking about it
   b. thinking about something
   c. organs

5. Why can't you see some of your body parts?
   They are on the inside of your body

6. Which body part pumps your blood?
   heart

Think about it: Make a list of all the inside body parts you can name. Try to think of what job each part does.

©1995 Kelley Wingate Publications, Inc.   26   KW 1012

Name _____ skill: comprehension

Heart

Your heart is an organ inside your chest. The heart is a muscle about the size of your fist. It works all the time without you thinking about it. Every time your heart beats, it pushes blood into your body. The blood goes to every part of your body (from head to toe) then comes back to the heart. This organ works harder than any other muscle you have. It works while you are awake or asleep. It works harder while you run or play. The heart never stops to rest!

1. What is the main idea of the story?
   a. The heart never stops.
   b. Blood goes to every part of a body.
   c. The heart is an organ.

2. How big is a heart?
   about the size of your fist.

3. Where is your heart?
   inside your chest

4. What job does the heart do?
   It pushes blood into your body.

5. What is the heart made of?
   muscle

6. When does the heart work very hard?
   while you run or play

Think about it: Find your heartbeat by putting your two middle fingers against your neck just under your jaw. Count the number of times your heart beats in one minute.

©1995 Kelley Wingate Publications, Inc.   27   KW 1012

Name _____ skill: comprehension

Lungs

You have two organs called lungs inside your chest. There is one on each side of your heart. Your lungs bring air into your body. As you breathe, or take in air, your chest gets bigger. That is because your lungs are filling with air. Their job is to take a gas called oxygen out of the air. Your body uses oxygen. You need it to live. Lungs get the oxygen from the air then send it to the rest of your body.

1. What is the main idea of this story?
   a. Lungs take oxygen from the air.
   b. Your chest gets bigger as you breathe in.
   c. Lungs are organs near your heart.

2. Where inside your body will you find the lungs?
   on each side of your heart

3. The word "breathe" means:
   a. live
   b. take in air
   c. lungs

4. What is oxygen?
   a gas in the air

5. Why does your chest get bigger when you breathe?
   because your lungs are filling with air.

6. What happens to the oxygen in your lungs?
   it sends it to the rest of your body

Think about it: Why do you think you need to take in new air every few seconds?

©1995 Kelley Wingate Publications, Inc.   28   KW 1012

Answer Key

Name _____

Stomach

You eat food everyday. The food you eat becomes energy for your body. You put the food into your mouth. Chewing helps break the food into smaller pieces. As you swallow, the food passes into your stomach. The stomach is an organ in the middle of your body. It is just below the heart and lungs. When food reaches the stomach it is broken into even smaller pieces. Some of the pieces are used to make energy for your body. The blood picks up these pieces and takes them to the rest of your body.

1. **What is the main idea of this story?**
   a. You must eat food to stay alive.
   b. Food is changed into energy.
   (c.) The stomach is an organ that changes food to help make energy.

2. **What does chewing do to food?**
   helps to break the food into smaller pieces.

3. **How does food get to your stomach?**
   It goes there after you swallow.

4. **What happens to food in your stomach?**
   It is broken into smaller pieces

5. **How do the pieces of food get to other parts of the body?**
   from the blood

6. **Why do we need to eat?**
   to give our bodies energy

Think about it: How do you think your teeth help your stomach?

©1995 Kelley Wingate Publications, Inc.   29   KW 1012

Name _____   skill: comprehension

Brain

Your brain is a very important organ inside your head. Your brain is where all thinking and learning takes place. The brain gets information, or facts, from your senses (eyes, ears, nose, mouth, and skin). Your brain tells your body what to do. When your ears hear someone call your name they send the sound to your brain. Your brain tells you to answer. Your brain also takes care of things you don't think about. It tells your lungs to breathe and your heart to beat. Your brain controls everything you do.

1. **What is the main idea of this story?**
   (a.) Your brain controls your body.
   b. The brain tells your heart to beat.
   c. The brain is an organ.

2. **Where is your brain?**
   Inside your head

3. **The word "information" means:**
   a. brain
   b. control
   (c.) facts

4. **Where does the brain get information?**
   from your senses

5. **What are the five senses?**
   sight, hearing, smell, taste, feel

6. **Why don't you have to think about breathing?**
   your brain tells your heart to beat

Think about it: What are other things your body does automatically?

©1995 Kelley Wingate Publications, Inc.   30   KW 1012

Name _____   skill: comprehension

Working Together

Each part of your body has a job to do. All the parts work together to help each other. The blood goes to every part of the body. It carries things your body needs. The blood gets oxygen in the lungs. It gets food in the stomach. It takes the food and oxygen to all the parts of your body. The brain gets food and oxygen through the blood. Food and oxygen help the brain work. The brain tells all the parts what to do. It makes sure all the parts work together. All the parts working together keep you alive and healthy, or well.

1. **What is the main idea of this story?**
   a. Each part of your body has a job.
   (b.) Body parts work together to keep us alive.
   c. Blood takes food to the rest of the body.

2. **How does the heart work with the stomach?**
   It gets food from the blood

3. **How do the lungs work with the stomach?**
   It pumps blood there.

4. **The word "healthy" means:**
   (a.) well, not sick
   b. alive
   c. working together

5. **How do the stomach and lungs help the brain?**
   food and oxygen help the brain work.

6. **How does the brain help other parts of the body?**
   It tells the parts what to do

Think about it: What would happen if any one body part does not do its job?

©1995 Kelley Wingate Publications, Inc.   31   KW 1012

Name _____   skill: comprehension

Staying Healthy

Your body works for you. It works to keep you alive and healthy. You must take care of your body so it can do its job. There are things you can do to help your body stay strong and healthy. You can exercise, drink water, eat good foods, and rest. Doing these things helps keep your body strong. Eating and drinking gives your body energy to do its job. Exercising and resting helps keep your body strong. When you do good things for your body, it is able to do the things you want it to. It is important to take care of your body.

1. **What is the main idea of this story?**
   (a.) You need to take care of your body.
   b. You must exercise.
   c. Resting is important.

2. **Name four things you should do for your body.**
   excercise, drink water, eat good foods, rest

3. **What does your body do for you?**
   It does the things you want it to

4. **Why should you take care of your body?**
   So it is able to do the things you want it to

5. **Why should you eat good foods?**
   to keep your body strong

Think about it: What might happen to your body if you did not take care of it?

©1995 Kelley Wingate Publications, Inc.   32   KW 1012

Answer Key

Name _____ skill: comprehension

Exercise and Rest

Exercise is one thing you can do to stay healthy. Muscles need to be used or they will become weak (not strong). Running, playing, and working helps make your muscles stronger. The more you use muscles, the stronger they will be. It is also important to get enough rest. As you exercise or use your muscles, you use energy. Resting gives your body a chance to relax and gather new energy. Children need even more sleep than grown-ups. Children are growing everyday, and growing takes a lot of energy. You need to work and play everyday. Be sure to get enough sleep, too!

1. **What is the main idea of this story?**
   a. Exercising makes muscles strong.
   b. It is important to get enough exercise and rest. (circled)
   c. Children need more rest than adults.
2. **What are some ways to make your muscles strong?**
   using your muscles through exercise
3. **The word "weak" means:**
   a. exercise
   b. sleep
   c. not strong (circled)
4. **How does exercise help you stay healthy?**
   it keeps your muscles strong
5. **How does resting help your body?**
   it gives your body a chance to get new energy
6. **Why do children need more sleep than grown-ups?**
   they use more energy

Think about it: Keep a list of things you do today that help make your muscles strong.

©1995 Kelley Wingate Publications, Inc.   33   KW 1012

Name _____ skill: comprehension

Germs

One thing you can do to help your body stay healthy is to keep yourself clean. You should wash your hands before you eat. You should take a bath everyday and keep your hair clean. You should keep your teeth clean by brushing them after you eat. Keeping your body clean is very important. Washing and being clean helps keep germs away. Germs are tiny little living things that you cannot see. They are in the air and on things we touch. Some germs can make you sick when they get inside your body. Keeping yourself clean helps kill germs and keeps you healthy.

1. **What is the main idea of this story?**
   a. Take a bath everyday.
   b. Germs can make you sick.
   c. Keeping clean can kill germs that make you sick. (circled)
2. **How can you keep your teeth clean?**
   by brushing them after you eat.
3. **What is a "germ"?**
   a. air
   b. tiny living things (circled)
   c. dirt
4. **Why is it important to keep yourself clean?**
   It helps keep germs away
5. **How can germs hurt you?**
   some germs can make you sick
6. **How can you keep yourself clean?**
   Washing, brushing your teeth

Think about it: Keep a list of things you do today that keep you clean.

©1995 Kelley Wingate Publications, Inc.   34   KW 1012

Name _____ skill: comprehension

Clothing

One way to help keep your body healthy is to wear the right clothes. You do not wear a heavy coat in the summer. You do not wear shorts in the winter. Your body needs to stay at the right temperature, or amount of heat. Wearing the right clothes helps keep you just the right temperature. During the summer when it is hot, we wear light clothes that let the heat escape, or get away from our body. During cold weather we wear hats, coats, and long pants that keep the heat in our bodies. Umbrellas and raincoats also help us. They keep our bodies dry. Getting wet cools our bodies. We wear rain clothes to help keep us warm and dry in wet weather. If we get too hot or too cold, our bodies have a hard time doing their jobs.

1. **What is the main idea of this story?**
   a. It is important to wear the right clothes. (circled)
   b. We wear shorts in the summer.
   c. Raincoats keep us dry.
2. **A word that means "amount of heat" is:**
   a. clothes
   b. temperature (circled)
   c. escape
3. **What warm things should we wear in the winter?**
   hats, coats, long pants
4. **Another word for "escape" is:**
   a. get away (circled)
   b. temperature
   c. dry
5. **Why do we wear cool clothes in the summer?**
   to let the heat escape
6. **What happens if your body is too warm or too cold?**
   Our body will have a hard time doing its job

Think about it: Draw a picture of yourself in winter and one in summer.

©1995 Kelley Wingate Publications, Inc.   35   KW 1012

Name _____ skill: comprehension

Food

Eating the right food is very important in keeping your body healthy. Your body uses food to make energy. Some foods are better for making energy than other foods. These good foods have things your body needs to grow strong and healthy. The Food Pyramid helps you choose good foods to eat. Dairy foods like milk and cheese are good for your bones and teeth. Meat and beans help build muscle. Fruits and vegetables give your body vitamins. Bread, cereal, rice, and pasta help give your body energy that will last a long time. A healthy meal will have foods from each of these pyramind groups.

1. **What is the main idea of this story?**
   a. Eating is fun.
   b. Milk helps your bones and teeth.
   c. Foods from the Food Pyramid give your body the things it needs to stay healthy. (circled)
2. **Why do you need to eat good foods?**
   Good foods keep the body healthy.
3. **Name foods from the Food Pyramid.**
   milk, cheese, meat, beans, fruit, vegetables, bread, cereal, rice, and pasta
4. **What kind of food helps muscles?**
   meat and beans
5. **What do fruits and vegetable give your body?**
   vitamins

© 1995 Kelley Wingate Publications, Inc.   36   CD-3709

Answer Key

Name _____ skill: comprehension

Taking Care of Your Teeth

Your teeth are very important to your health. Without strong teeth you cannot eat the foods that your body needs. Food can get stuck between your teeth. Sugar coats your teeth. The food and sugar can put holes called cavities in your teeth. You should brush your teeth every morning and every night. Brushing well gets food and sugar off your teeth. Two times a year you should visit your dentist, a doctor who takes care of teeth. The dentist will clean your teeth and fill any cavities you might have.

1. What is the main idea of this story?
   a. Teeth help us eat.
   b. It is important to take care of your teeth.
   c. A dentist checks your teeth.
2. Why do we need strong healthy teeth?
   So we can eat the foods our body needs
3. The word "cavity" means:
   a. a hole in a tooth
   b. a doctor
   c. strong teeth
4. What can give you cavities?
   food and sugar
5. What can you do to keep your teeth healthy?
   brush your teeth, go to the dentist
6. How do dentists help our teeth?
   they clean your teeth, fix any cavities

Think about it: Count how many teeth you have. How many fillings do your have (cavities that have been fixed)? Compare your answers with other people in the class.

©1995 Kelley Wingate Publications, Inc.   37   KW 1012

Name _____ skill: comprehension

Checkups

Each year you should visit your doctor for a checkup. A checkup is when the doctor sees how well you are growing. The doctor will see how much weight you have gained. She will measure how tall you are to make sure you are growing as you should. The doctor will check many parts of your body. She will look in your ears and listen to your heart to see if you have any health problems. A checkup can help the doctor find any problems that may be beginning. A checkup makes sure that you stay healthy!

1. What is the main idea of this story?
   a. A checkup keeps you healthy.
   b. The doctor checks your weight.
   c. The doctor may find problems that are beginning.
2. How many times a year should you have a checkup?
   Once
3. What is a checkup?
   The doctor sees how well you are growing
4. How can the doctor tell if you are growing as you should?
   check your weight, see how tall you are
5. What will the doctor do to you during a checkup?
   check many parts of your body
6. What is the doctor looking for during a checkup?
   he makes sure you stay healthy

Think about it: Find out when your last checkup was.

©1995 Kelley Wingate Publications, Inc.   38   KW 1012

Name _____ skill: comprehension

Medicine

Sometimes you go to the doctor when you are sick. The doctor tells you what is wrong. She gives you medicine, something that helps make you well. The medicine can be a shot, pills, or something you drink. No one likes to take medicine, but it helps make you healthy again. Sometimes during a checkup the doctor will give you medicine that helps keep you from getting sick. This medicine is called a vaccine. A vaccine can keep you from getting measles, mumps, and other illnesses. Taking medicine when you need it will help you get better. Taking good care of your body all the time will help you stay healthy.

1. What is the main idea of this story?
   a. Medicine helps make you healthy.
   b. No one likes to take medicine.
   c. Some medicines keep you from getting sick.
2. "Medicine" is:
   a. a shot
   b. something that makes you feel better when you are sick
   c. illness
3. Name three ways you can take medicine.
   shots, pills, something you drink
4. A word that means "medicine that keeps you healthy" is:
   a. vaccine
   b. measles
   c. illness
5. Why do doctors give you vaccines?
   to keep you from getting sick
6. Why do we take medicine?
   to help you get better

Think about it: If you take care of yourself and get vaccines will you ever get sick? Explain what you think and why.

©1995 Kelley Wingate Publications, Inc.   39   KW 1012

Name _____ skill: comprehension

Animals

Animals are living things that can move and reproduce, or make new animals. There are many kinds of animals. Man is an animal. Birds are animals. A snail is an animal. Even bees and ants are animals. All animals need to eat. They eat plants or other animals to give them energy, or strength. All animals need to be safe. They build homes to protect themselves from weather and other animals.

1. What is the main idea of this story?
   a. Man is an animal.
   b. Animals build homes.
   c. Animals are living things.
2. Name four animals.
   Man, birds, snail, bees
3. The word reproduce means:
   a. animals
   b. make new animals
   c. keep safe
4. Another word for energy is:
   a. strength
   b. protect
   c. snail
5. Why do animals need to eat?
   to get energy
6. Why do animals need to build homes?
   to protect themselves

Think about it: Can you name four animals that are not in this story?

©1995 Kelley Wingate Publications, Inc.   40   KW 1012

Answer Key

Name _____ skill: comprehension

Extinct

Many kinds of animals are extinct, all of their kind have died. Dinosaurs are extinct. There are no more dinosaurs alive on the earth. Scientists, people who study nature, are not sure what killed them. Some animals are extinct because the land where they lived changed. Others are extinct because hunters killed too many of them. When an animal becomes extinct it is gone forever.

1. **What is the main idea of this story?**
   a. Some animals are extinct. *(circled)*
   b. Dinosaurs are extinct.
   c. Hunters kill animals.
2. **Why are dinosaurs extinct?**
   people are not sure why
3. **The word "extinct" means:**
   a. all of those animals are dead *(circled)*
   b. not sure
   c. almost all of those animals are dead
4. **A word that means "people who study the earth" is:**
   a. extinct
   b. nature
   c. scientist *(circled)*
5. **What two things can make an animal extinct?**
   Land changes, hunters
6. **How can we get extinct animals to come back?**
   we can't

Think about it: What can we do to make sure no more animals become extinct?

©1995 Kelley Wingate Publications, Inc.　　41　　KW 1012

Name _____ skill: comprehension

Endangered

Some kinds of animals are in trouble. There are not many left and they many become extinct. These animals are endangered, or in danger of becoming extinct. The bald eagles are endangered. They were hunted for many years. The panda is another endangered animal. It lives in the forests of China. Many of the forests have been cleared, or cut for the wood and land. Now the pandas have less space and less food. Some people are trying to help endangered animals. There are laws to keep endangered animals safe.

1. **What is the main idea of this story?**
   a. Pandas live in China.
   b. Some animals are close to being extinct. *(circled)*
   c. Laws help endangered animals.
2. **A word that means "in danger of becoming extinct" is:**
   a. extinct
   b. endangered *(circled)*
   c. panda
3. **Why are bald eagles endangered?**
   They were hunted for many years
4. **Another word for cleared is:**
   a. cut down *(circled)*
   b. space
   c. land
5. **Why is the panda endangered?**
   They have less space and less food
6. **What are people doing to help endangered animals?**
   making laws to keep endangered animals safe

Think about it: How can we help endangered animals?

©1995 Kelley Wingate Publications, Inc.　　42　　KW 1012

Name _____ skill: comprehension

Plants

Plants are living things. They can grow and reproduce. Most plants grow from seeds. When the plant gets big it makes new seeds. It is called a parent plant. A nut is a seed. A flower makes seeds. A seed needs three things to grow. It needs water, air, and a warm place to grow. Most seeds are planted in the spring. It is warm in the spring, and there is more water in the soil.

1. **What is the main idea of this story?**
   a. Plants are living things. *(circled)*
   b. A flower makes seeds.
   c. It is warm in the spring.
2. **How do new plants start?**
   from seeds
3. **What is a parent plant?**
   it makes seeds
4. **What is a seed?**
   it grows into a new plant
5. **What three things do seeds need to begin growing?**
   water, air, warm place
6. **When are most seeds planted?**
   spring

Think about it: Name three things that have seeds.

©1995 Kelley Wingate Publications, Inc.　　43　　KW 1012

Name _____ skill: comprehension

How Seeds Grow

A new plant grows from a seed. The seed has a tough, or hard, outside part called the seed coat. Inside the seed coat is the new plant. There is also food for the new plant stored inside the seed coat. As the new plant eats the stored food and begins to grow, the seed coat splits so the plant can come out. A tiny new plant is called a seedling. It looks like its parent plant, but is much smaller. When it uses up all the stored food, the seedling will make its own food. Seedlings make their food from water, air, and light.

1. **What is the main idea of this story?**
   a. New plants look like the parent plant.
   b. The seed coat protects the new plant.
   c. Seeds grow into seedlings. *(circled)*
2. **A word that means hard is:**
   a. split
   b. stored
   c. tough *(circled)*
3. **What is a seed coat?**
   The outside part of a seed
4. **A new plant is called a:**
   a. seed coat
   b. seedling *(circled)*
   c. split
5. **What is inside a seed coat?**
   a new plant
6. **What do seedlings need to make their own food?**
   water, air, light

Think about it: Open an apple or orange seed. Find the seed coat, stored food, and new plant inside.

©1995 Kelley Wingate Publications, Inc.　　44　　KW 1012

Answer Key

Name _____ skill: comprehension

Parts of a Plant

Most plants have roots, stems, and leaves. Each part helps the plant in a special way. Roots are under the soil. They hold the plant so it can grow. Roots get water from the soil and give it to the plant. Stems are the body of the plant. They can be tall or short, hard or soft. Stems hold the leaves up to get light. They carry water from the roots to the leaves. Leaves make the food for the plant. They use air and light to make food. All three parts are important to plants.

1. **What is the main idea of this story?**
   (a.) Plants have three parts.
   b. Leaves make food for the plant.
   c. Roots hold the plant up.
2. **What do roots do?**
   hold the plant
3. **Which part of a plant holds up the leaves?**
   a. roots
   (b.) stem
   c. leaves
4. **What does the stem do?**
   Carry water from the roots to the leaves
5. **What do the leaves do?**
   make food for the plant
6. **Why does a plant need all three parts?**
   they are all important

Think about it: Draw a picture of a plant. Label the roots, stem, and leaves.

©1995 Kelley Wingate Publications, Inc.   45   KW 1012

Name _____ skill: comprehension

How We Use Plants

People need plants. Trees give us wood that we use to build things. Trees also give us shade and help us stay cool in warm weather. People eat many kinds of plants. We eat some roots. Onions, beets, and carrots are plant roots. We eat stems. Celery is a plant stem. We eat leaves. Spinach and lettuce are plant leaves. We also eat seeds. Nuts and berries are plant seeds. When we eat these plant parts, we are getting the food the plant has stored for itself.

1. **What is the main idea of this story?**
   a. Trees help us in many ways.
   b. Plant parts taste good.
   (c.) People use plants in many ways.
2. **How do trees help us?**
   Wood for building, shade to stay cool
3. **What parts of plants do we eat?**
   roots, stems, leaves
4. **Name three roots that we eat.**
   onions, beets, carrots
5. **Name two kinds of leaves that we eat.**
   spinach, lettuce
6. **What do we get when we eat plants?**
   the food the plant has stored for itself

Think about it: Make a list of foods we get from plant roots, stems, leaves, and seeds.

©1995 Kelley Wingate Publications, Inc.   46   KW 1012

Name _____ skill: comprehension

Flowers and Fruit

Most plants have flowers that make their seeds. The flower petals come in many shapes and bright colors. Some flowers are tiny and hard to find. Others are very large and pretty. The seeds of these plants are made inside the flowers. When the seeds are ready, the petals dry up and fall off. The part of the flower that holds the seeds gets bigger. This part grows and becomes the fruit. Apples and oranges are fruits that grow from flowers. The fruit has the plant seeds inside.

1. **What is the main idea of this story?**
   a. Many seeds come from plant flowers.
   (b.) Many plants have flowers.
   c. Fruit has seeds.
2. **What do flowers make?**
   seeds
3. **What color and shape are flower petals?**
   many shapes and bright colors
4. **What happens to the flower when the seeds are ready?**
   it dries up and falls off
5. **What is inside the fruit?**
   plant seeds
6. **Name two kinds of fruit.**
   apples, oranges

Think about it: Can you name three other kinds of fruit?

©1995 Kelley Wingate Publications, Inc.   47   KW 1012

Name _____ skill: comprehension

Nuts and Cones

Some plants do not have flowers or fruit. They have nuts or cones to make new seeds. Walnuts, acorns, and almonds are nuts. The new plant and its stored food are inside a hard shell. As the seed begins to grow, the shell cracks open so the new plant can get bigger. Other plants, like the pine tree, have cones that hold their seeds. The cones are hard on the outside. This keeps the seeds safe inside. There are many seeds inside one cone. When the seeds are ready, the cone opens and they fall out.

1. **What is the main idea of this story?**
   a. A pine tree has seeds in a cone.
   (b.) Some plants have seeds inside nuts or cones.
   c. Some plants do not have flowers or fruit.
2. **What are the three parts of a nut?**
   the new plant, stored food, and a hard shell.
3. **How does the new plant get out of a nut?**
   the shell cracks
4. **What is inside a pine cone?**
   seeds
5. **What happens when a cone opens?**
   the seeds fall out
6. **Name three kinds of nuts that are seeds for plants.**
   walnuts, acorns, almonds

Think about it: Make a list of plants that have nuts or cones for seeds.

©1995 Kelley Wingate Publications, Inc.   48   KW 1012

Answer Key

Name _____ skill: comprehension

How Seeds Travel

A parent plant makes a lot of seeds. The seeds must leave the parent and get into the soil before they can grow. Some seeds just drop from the parent plant. Other seeds travel, or go far away, before they grow. The wind carries some kinds of seeds. Other seeds are sticky or have hooks that help them stick to animals that pass by. The animal may carry the seeds a long way before they fall off and find their way into the soil. Some seeds can float, or ride on top of water. The water carries these seeds far from the parent plant before they find a place to grow. Only a few seeds will grow. Many never find a place that has enough water or light. Others are eaten by animals. If every seed found a place to grow, the world would have too many plants!

1. What is the main idea of this story?
   a. Seeds must find a good place to grow.
   b. The wind carries some seeds to new places.
   c. Animals eat many seeds.
2. Name three ways that seeds can travel.
   Drop, wind, animals, float
3. A word that means "to stay on top of water" is:
   a. seed
   b. travel
   c. float
4. How do animals help seeds?
   they carry them.
5. How do animals stop seeds from growing?
   they eat them.

Think about it: What would happen if every seed found a place to grow?

©1995 Kelley Wingate Publications, Inc.   49   KW 1012

Name _____ skill: comprehension

Matter

Plants take up space. Animals take up space. Nonliving things, things that are not alive, take up space, too. Things that take up space are called matter. Look around your room. Can you see matter? The desks are matter. The books are matter. Even the teacher is matter! Matter can be put into three groups. They are called states of matter, or kinds of matter. These states are solid, liquid, and gas. All matter is in one of these states. Some matter can change from one state to another. Water is matter that can be in any of the states. Water is a liquid. When it is frozen it becomes a solid. When water becomes very hot it turns into steam, which is a gas. All three states take up space. All three states are forms of matter.

1. What is the main idea of this story?
   a. Water is liquid matter.
   b. Matter is anything that takes up space.
   c. Gas is matter.
2. What is matter?
   Anything that takes up space
3. A word that means "not alive" is:
   a. nonliving
   b. matter
   c. states of matter
4. Another word for "states" is:
   a. kinds
   b. nonliving
   c. liquid
5. What are the three states of matter?
   Solid, liquid, gas

Think about it: Make a list of kinds of matter you can find in your classroom.

©1995 Kelley Wingate Publications, Inc.   50   KW 1012

Name _____ skill: comprehension

Volume and Mass

Which takes up more space, an ant or a table? The table does because it is bigger than the ant. The size of the space something takes up is called volume. Things that take up space can be heavy or light. An elephant is heavy. A piece of paper that is taller than the elephant is light. The elephant has more mass. Mass is the amount of matter something has. Think of two boxes that are the same size. One box is filled with feathers. The other box is filled with books. They both have the same volume, or size. The box with the books is heavier. It has more mass than the box with the feathers.

1. What is the main idea of this story?
   a. Things can be heavy or light.
   b. Books are heavier than feathers.
   c. Matter has volume and mass.
2. A word that means "the amount of space taken" is:
   a. mass
   b. volume
   c. heavy
3. Are bigger things always heavier than smaller things?
   No
4. What does the word "mass" mean?
   a. the size of something
   b. feathers
   c. the amount of matter something has
5. Which has more volume, a pencil or a book?
   Book
6. Which has more mass, a gallon of water or a gallon of air?
   Water

Think about it: Make a list of things that have a lot of volume but not much mass.

©1995 Kelley Wingate Publications, Inc.   51   KW 1012

Name _____ skill: comprehension

Solid

There are three kinds of matter. They are called solid, liquid, and gas. Solid matter will keep its shape even when it is moved. A pencil is solid. It looks the same on your desk or in your hand. It does not change its shape. Solids can be soft, too. A shirt is a soft solid. It can bend and move with you, but it does not change its shape. The shirt will never look like a box or a ball. It will always have the shape of a shirt. A solid will have the same shape, volume, and mass any place you put it. It does not change by itself.

1. What is the main idea of this story?
   a. Solid matter does not change from place to place.
   b. A pencil is a solid.
   c. A shirt is a soft solid.
2. What happens to a solid's shape when you move it?
   It stays the same
3. Circle the things in the list below that are solid matter.
   cup   water   book   chair
   doll   tree   milk   cream
   coat   car   person   juice
4. What three things will stay the same anywhere the solid matter goes?
   Pencil, box, ball
5. Are all solids hard? Explain.
   No. Some are soft, like a shirt.

Think about it: Make a list of solid matter you can find in your classroom.

©1995 Kelley Wingate Publications, Inc.   52   KW 1012

Answer Key

Name _____ skill: comprehension

Liquid

One kind of matter is liquid. Liquid matter does not have a shape at all. Water is a liquid. It does not have its own shape. It will take the shape of whatever you put it in. Measure one cup of water and pour it into a tall glass. The water now has the shape of the glass. If you pour that water into a bowl, it spreads out and takes the shape of the bowl. The amount of water, or volume, has not changed. You had one cup in the glass and the same cup of water in the bowl. The shape of the water did change. A liquid will change its shape when it is moved, but it does not change volume or mass. It will be the same amount and weight no matter where you put it.

1. **What is the main idea of this story?**
   a. Liquid is a matter that changes shape.
   b. Water is a liquid.
   c. Liquids are a kind of matter.
2. **What is a liquid?**
   Matter that does not have a shape.
3. **What happens to water when you move it from one place to another?**
   It changes shape.
4. **Circle the things in the list below that are liquid matter .**

   cup   water   book   tea
   doll   tree   car   bread
   cola   milk   person   juice

5. **What stays the same when a liquid is moved?**
   the volume or amount

Think about it: Make a list of liquid matter you can find in your home or classroom.

©1995 Kelley Wingate Publications, Inc.   53   KW 1012

Name _____ skill: comprehension

Gas

The third kind of matter is called gas. Gas, like liquid, does not have a shape. Air is a gas. It takes the shape of whatever you put it in. Blow air into a balloon. The air takes the shape of the balloon. Put air into a bicycle tire. It takes the shape of the tire. Gas can change its volume, or size, too. If you put the balloon in a cool place over night, it will be smaller in the morning. The air did not leak out. It became smaller! The air can expand, or get bigger, if it is warmed. Gas does not have a shape and it can change its volume.

1. **What is the main idea of this story?**
   a. Air will take the shape of a balloon.
   b. Gas is a type of matter.
   c. Gas has no shape.
2. **What happens to a gas when you move it to a new place?**
   It changes shape.
3. **What happens to a gas if it is heated or cooled?**
   It gets bigger or smaller
4. **What word means "to get bigger"?**
   a. gas
   b. leak
   c. expand
5. **How is gas different from solid?**
   It can change shape
6. **How is gas different from liquid?**
   It can get bigger or smaller

Think about it: Make a chart that tells about solids, liquids, and gases. List things that belong to each group.

©1995 Kelley Wingate Publications, Inc.   54   KW 1012

Name _____ skill: comprehension

Community

People live together in groups. They help each other everyday. We live in towns or cities where people help each other by doing their jobs. We do not grow our own food. We do not make our own clothes. Other people have the jobs of getting food and clothes in their stores so we can buy them. These types of jobs give us goods, or products we need. Other people have service jobs. These service jobs do things we do not have time to do ourselves. People who mow lawns, clean clothes, or cut hair provide services. When people live near each other and help each other they are called a community. The town or city where you live is a community.

1. **What is the main idea of this story?**
   a. The grocer gives us food.
   b. We live in communities to help each other.
   c. Some jobs give a service.
2. **Why do we live in communities?**
   So people can help each other
3. **Another word for goods is:**
   a. products
   b. services
   c. nice people
4. **Another word for service is:**
   a. watch
   b. important
   c. do things for others
5. **Why do people need to help each other?**
   To get different jobs done.
6. **What is a community?**
   People living together in a group.

Think about it: Can you name three other service jobs?

©1995 Kelley Wingate Publications, Inc.   55   KW 1012

Name _____ skill: comprehension

Police

One service job we see almost everyday is a policeman. The police in our community have many jobs to do. They watch the roads to see that people drive safely. They give tickets if we drive too fast or break the rules of the road. Police also look for people who are breaking other laws. They try to protect us from robbers and other bad people. Police also help in other ways. If we get lost they can help us find our way home. Police make sure that people obey the laws that keep us safe.

1. **What is the main idea of this story?**
   a. Police give tickets.
   b. Police help lost people.
   c. Police have service jobs.
2. **Why do police watch the roads?**
   To see that people drive safely
3. **Another word for protect is:**
   a. keep us safe
   b. hide
   c. stop
4. **How can police help us?**
   Protect us, find our way if lost
5. **What do police do if someone drives too fast?**
   Give a ticket
6. **What is another word for obey?**
   a. drive safely
   b. follow the rules
   c. keep safe

Think about it: Can you name three other service jobs?

©1995 Kelley Wingate Publications, Inc.   56   KW 1012

Answer Key

Name _____ skill: comprehension

Firefighters

One service job we all know is the firefighter. The firefighter drives a big red truck. A firefighter wears a large hat and a heavy coat. A firefighter's job is to put out fires. In big cities the firefighters live in the firehouse so they are ready to go at all times. They take turns cooking dinner and keeping the firehouse clean. In some towns the firefighters are volunteers. They are usually not paid and do the job because they want to help. They have other jobs and are firefighters only when there is a fire. When an alarm sounds, these firefighters leave their jobs and go to the firehouse. Both kinds of firefighters help keep our homes and businesses safe.

1. **What is the main idea of this story?**
   a. Firefighters work in the city.
   b. Firefighters are ready anytime.
   c. Firefighters help protect us from fires.
2. **What does a firefighter do?**
   Put out fires
3. **What does a firefighter wear?**
   A large hat and heavy coat
4. **Where do big city firefighters live?**
   In the firehouse
5. **What does volunteer mean?**
   a. not paid for work
   b. firehouse
   c. has another job
6. **How do volunteer firefighters know when there is a fire?**
   An alarm sounds

Think about it: Why do city firefighters need to live at the firehouse?

©1995 Kelley Wingate Publications, Inc.   57   KW 1012

Name _____ skill: comprehension

Doctor

A doctor helps people who are sick or hurt. Doctors go to school for many years to learn how our bodies work. They study many subjects and work in hospitals to learn how to make people well. Some doctors specialize, or become an expert, in one thing. They may take care of just hearts, eyes, bones, or other parts of the body. Doctors also learn about medicine or drugs. They know what to give us to help make us well again. Doctors are an important part of our community. They help to keep all of us well.

1. **What is the main idea of this story?**
   a. Doctors keep us well.
   b. Some doctors take care of hearts.
   c. Doctors learn about medicine.
2. **What do doctors learn about in school?**
   How our bodies work
3. **What is a doctor's job?**
   To help people who are sick
4. **What is a word that means specialize?**
   a. to be important
   b. teach
   c. become an expert
5. **What is a word that means drugs?**
   a. specialize
   b. medicine
   c. body
6. **Why are doctors important to a community?**
   They help keep us well and help us when we become sick or hurt.

Think about it: Why might you go to see a doctor?

©1995 Kelley Wingate Publications, Inc.   58   KW 1012

Name _____ skill: comprehension

Dentist

Sometimes people have a problem with their teeth. They may get a cavity in their tooth. A cavity is a hole that can be painful if it is not taken care of. Special doctors called dentists take care of our teeth. We should see a dentist two times each year. The dentist will clean our teeth and look for problems during this checkup. This helps keep our teeth and gums healthy. If you have a toothache or cavity, the dentist can fix the problem. As people get older they may lose some teeth. A dentist can make false teeth called dentures for them to wear. A dentist has the job of keeping our teeth clean and healthy.

1. **What is the main idea of this story?**
   a. Dentists fill cavities.
   b. Dentists make dentures.
   c. Dentists keep our teeth clean and healthy.
2. **Another word for a hole in your tooth is:**
   a. denture
   b. cavity
   c. dentist
3. **Why should we visit the dentist twice a year?**
   To clean our teeth and look for problems.
4. **Name two things a dentist can help you with.**
   Keep our gums and teeth healthy
   Fix a toothache or cavity
5. **How does a dentist help our community?**
   Helps keep our teeth healthy.

Think about it: Tell about the last time you went to see your dentist.

©1995 Kelley Wingate Publications, Inc.   59   KW 1012

Name _____ skill: comprehension

Farmer

Farmers are a part of a community. Most people do not have enough time to grow their own food. A farmer's job is to grow food or raise animals for others to buy. Some farmers plant many acres, or fields, with different fruits, vegetables, or grains. Other farmers raise animals that are used for food or material. Cows can be used for meat, leather, and dairy products like milk and cheese. Chickens are raised for meat, eggs, and feathers. Pigs give us meat and leather. Sheep are used for their meat and wool. Each farmer helps feed the community or provides the animals to make the products we buy.

1. **What is the main idea of this story?**
   a. Farmers provide food and materials for products.
   b. Farmers raise cows.
   c. Meat, leather, and dairy products come from cows.
2. **Why don't most people grow their own food?**
   They do not have enough time.
3. **What products do we get from cows?**
   Milk, butter, meat, cheese
4. **A word that means "large fields" is:**
   a. acres
   b. farm
   c. dairy products
5. **From which animal do we get wool?**
   Sheep
6. **How do farmers help the community?**
   They provide food and products

Think about it: Name three farm products your family uses.

©1995 Kelley Wingate Publications, Inc.   60   KW 1012

Answer Key

Name _____ skill: comprehension

Grocer

Most people in communities do not have time to go to farms to get their food. They buy food in places called grocery stores. The owner of a grocery store is called a grocer. He buys fresh fruit and vegetables from farmers. He buys canned and boxed foods from food packaging factories. Then he puts the food on shelves in his store and sells it to our families. The grocer offers many foods that we could not grow ourselves. He saves us time by gathering together different foods so we can go to one place to buy what we need.

1. **What is the main idea of this story?**
   a. Grocers buy food from farmers.
   b. People do not have time to go to farms.
   c. Grocers help us by gathering food in one place.
2. **Where do vegetables and fruits come from?**
   Farms
3. **Where do canned goods come from?**
   Food packaging factories
4. **What is a word that means "grocery store owner"?**
   a. grocer
   b. farm
   c. packaging factory
5. **What happens to food at a packaging factory?**
   It is put into cans and boxes
6. **Why is a grocer so important to a community?**
   He saves us time.

Think about it: Tell what things your family often gets at a grocery store.

Name _____ skill: comprehension

Neighbors

The people that live near us are called neighbors. If you live in an apartment, the people in your building are your neighbors. If you live in a house, the people on your block are your neighbors. You see your neighbors during the day as they come and go or work in their yards. Neighbors know your name and help you in many ways. When you go on vacation a neighbor might pick up your mail or newspaper for you. They keep watch on your home to see that no one bothers it while you are away. Neighbors often borrow things from each other. The people in the neighborhood help protect each other.

1. **What is the main idea of this story?**
   a. Neighbors help each other.
   b. Neighbors borrow things.
   c. A neighborhood is nice.
2. **Tell three ways neighbors help each other:**
   Pick up mail or newspapers
   Watch our home.
   Borrow things.
3. **If you live in a house, who are your neighbors?**
   The people on my block.
4. **Where might you see your neighbor?**
   As they come and go or in their yard
5. **Why are neighbors important to a community?**
   They help protect each other.

Think about it: Name two of your neighbors.

Name _____ skill: comprehension

Restaurant

A community has many different people that help us in some way. It also has many businesses where we can buy goods. One business you can find in every community is a restaurant. A restaurant is a store that sells food that is ready to eat. Some restaurants sell fast food, or meals that you can get very quickly. They usually have a drive-through window so you can pick up food without getting out of your car. Other restaurants are dine in. You go inside these restaurants, sit at a table, and get waited on. You order from a menu, a list of food, and it is cooked while you wait. The people that take your order and bring the food are called waiters or waitresses. A restaurant helps us by serving food when we don't have time to cook for ourselves.

1. **What is the main idea of this story?**
   a. Waiters bring you food.
   b. A restaurant helps people who are too busy to cook.
   c. Fast food tastes good.
2. **What is a restaurant?**
   a store that sells food that is ready to eat
3. **What is "fast food"?**
   meals we can get very quickly
4. **A restaurant that serves food at a table is called:**
   a. fast food
   b. waiter
   c. dine in
5. **Waiter and waitress are names of people who:**
   a. serve you food
   b. own restaurants
   c. sell food

Think about it: What is the name of your favorite restaurant?

Name _____ skill: comprehension

School

One very important part of every community is a school. School is a place where people become educated about the world. There are a few different kinds of schools. Elementary, junior high, and high schools are places where children go to learn math, reading, history, and science. After high school, some people go to trade school where they can learn skills for becoming a secretary or truck driver. Other people choose to go to college. College takes at least four years and prepares you for professional jobs like doctor, lawyer, or scientist. Without schools it would be hard to learn what we need to know to get a good job.

1. **What is the main idea of this story?**
   a. Schools teach us about the world.
   b. Trade schools teach skills.
   c. You can't get a job without school.
2. **What three types of schools educate children?**
   Elementary, junior high, high school
3. **What school teaches job skills?**
   trade
4. **What school prepares you for a profession?**
   college
5. **What does educate mean?**
   a. school
   b. professional
   c. learn
6. **Why are schools important to a community?**
   People learn what they need to know

Think about it: What job would you like? What school will help you prepare for this job?

Answer Key

Name _____ skill: comprehension

Library

A library is a place where you can borrow books to read. The library has many different kinds of books. There are fiction books to read for fun. There are how-to books that explain how to do things like fix a bike or make a model rocket. Reference books are full of facts we might want to know more about. A person called a librarian keeps the books in order and helps us find what we are looking for. We can borrow books for a week or two, but we must return them so others can use them, too. You need a library card in order to borrow books. The librarian can help you get one.

1. **What is the main idea of this story?**
   (a.) You can find many books in a library.
   b. Librarians help you find books.
   c. You need a library card.
2. **What is a library?**
   a place where we can borrow books
3. **Name three kinds of books you can find in a library.**
   fiction, how-to, reference
4. **Why must you return the books?**
   so others can read them, too
5. **The person who works in the library is a:**
   a. teacher
   b. book
   (c.) librarian
6. **Why are libraries important to a community?**
   they hold information

Think about it: What is the name of your school librarian?

©1995 Kelley Wingate Publications, Inc.   65   KW 1012

Name _____ skill: comprehension

Hospital

Every large community has a hospital. A hospital is a place where people go when they are very sick or hurt. Doctors and nurses work there. If your tonsils hurt, you might go to a hospital to have them taken out. The doctor will put you to sleep then take you to the operating room. This is a very clean room where doctors remove or fix things inside your body. When someone gets hurt in an accident, they are taken to a hospital where they can be helped. Most hospitals also have a nursery. That is the place where babies are kept for the first few days after birth. The hospital nursery takes care of new babies and makes sure that they are healthy. Hospitals do a good job of helping the community stay healthy!

1. **What is the main idea of this story?**
   a. A hospital is a very clean place.
   (b.) Hospitals help very sick or hurt people.
   c. Hospitals have a nursery for babies.
2. **Who works in a hospital?**
   Doctors and nurses
3. **When might someone go to a hospital?**
   when they are sick or hurt
4. **What is an operating room?**
   a clean room where doctors fix our bodies
5. **What is a room for babies?**
   a. operating room
   (b.) nursery
   c. hospital
6. **How are hospitals important to a community?**
   they help us stay healthy

Think about it: Tell about a time when you were in or visited a hospital.

©1995 Kelley Wingate Publications, Inc.   66   KW 1012

Name _____ skill: comprehension

Department Store

A department store is a large place that sells many different goods. A department is a group or area of things that are alike. There are clothes, tool, toy, garden, shoe, and kitchen departments all in the same store. If you need a pair of shoes and a hammer you do not need to go to a clothes store and a hardware store. You can get both things in one stop at a department store. This kind of shopping takes less time and is easy or convenient for most people.

1. **What is the main idea of this story?**
   (a.) Department stores make shopping easier.
   b. Shoes and hammers are sold together.
   c. A store is convenient.
2. **What is a department store?**
   a large place that sells different goods
3. **What is another name for an area where things are alike?**
   a. same
   b. store
   (c.) department
4. **What word in the story means easy?**
   (a.) convenient
   b. shopping
   c. department
5. **What departments might you find in a department store?**
   clothes, toys, tool, garden, shoe kitchen
6. **How does a department store help a community?**
   It makes shopping take less time

Think about it: Name a department store you have been to.

©1995 Kelley Wingate Publications, Inc.   67   KW 1012

Name _____ skill: comprehension

Gas Station

An important business for any community is a gas station. This is a place where we can get gasoline for our cars and trucks. A gas station can also fix your vehicle if it is not working right. They have pumps to put air in bicycle or car tires. They sell maps of the city or state to help you on the road. Some gas stations even have a car wash to keep your vehicle clean! This business is important because we use our cars or trucks everyday. If your car is broken or out of gas you cannot go very far from home.

1. **What is the main idea of this story?**
   a. Gas stations sell gasoline.
   (b.) A gas station helps keep our vehicles running.
   c. We can buy maps at a gas station.
2. **What is a gas station?**
   where we get gas for our vehicles
3. **Name four things you can get or do at a gas station:**
   Gasoline
   air
   buy maps
   wash our cars
4. **What is another word for cars and trucks?**
   a. pumps
   (b.) vehicles
   c. bicycles
5. **Why are gas stations important to a community?**
   they help us use our vehicles every day

Think about it: Draw a picture of the gas station you go to.

©1995 Kelley Wingate Publications, Inc.   68   KW 1012

Answer Key

Name _____ skill: comprehension

Park

Every community usually has a park for people to use. A park is an area set aside for recreation, or fun activities. There is a playground for children. It has swings, slides, or monkey bars to play on. Many parks have football fields, baseball diamonds, soccer fields, and a track for running. You can find picnic tables to sit on while you eat your lunch or dinner. Many parks have trees and a pond or lake to enjoy. A park is where people of the community can relax and have fun when they are not at school or work.

1. **What is the main idea of this story?**
   a. Parks are places were people relax. *(circled)*
   b. You can eat your lunch at a table.
   c. People don't like to work.
2. **What is a park?**
   a place to relax and play
3. **Name three things you might do at a park:**
   swing, slide, climb, play sports, picnic

4. **What is another word for fun activities?**
   a. parks
   b. relax
   c. recreation *(circled)*
5. **How are parks important to a community?**
   they are places to relax and have fun

Think about it: Draw a picture of yourself at a park.

©1995 Kelley Wingate Publications, Inc.   69   KW 1012

Name _____ skill: comprehension
Read the story.

Craig and Ernie

Mother gives Craig and his friend Ernie some chocolate cake. Craig thinks chocolate cake is the best kind of cake, but thinks that yellow cake is even better. They eat all of the cake. Now they are thirsty and want some milk. They both agree that white milk is better than chocolate milk!

Tell whether each sentence is a fact (F) or an opinion (O):

F — Mother gave Craig and Ernie some chocolate cake.

O — Chocolate cake is the best kind of cake.

F — Ernie likes yellow cake better than chocolate cake.

O — Yellow cake is better than chocolate cake.

F — Craig and Ernie drank a glass of white milk.

O — White milk is better than chocolate milk.

Write one fact about this story.
answers will vary

Write one opinion about this story.
answers will vary

©1995 Kelley Wingate Publications, Inc.   70   KW 1012

Name _____ skill: comprehension
Read the story.

Vinnie

Vinnie loves children. He tells good jokes and makes up great stories for them. Children like Vinnie, too. They think he tells the best stories they have ever heard. They like to laugh at his silly jokes. Once Vinnie told a joke and then laughed so hard he fell off his chair. The children thought that was very funny. Vinnie didn't!

Tell whether each sentence is a fact (F) or an opinion (O):

F — Vinnie loves children.

F — Vinnie tells jokes and stories.

F — Children like Vinnie.

O — He tells stories better than anyone else.

F — Vinnie fell off his chair.

O — His fall was very funny.

Write one fact about this story.
answers will vary

Write one opinion about this story.
answers will vary

©1995 Kelley Wingate Publications, Inc.   71   KW 1012

Name _____ skill: comprehension
Read the story.

Which is Better?

The teacher let us draw pictures today. I drew a big blue flower. Patty drew a lot of little yellow flowers. Val drew three purple birds. The teacher said that all three drawings were very nice. Patty thinks that her picture is really prettier than mine. Val says that hers is the nicest. I am sure that mine is really the best of all.

Tell whether each sentence is a fact (F) or an opinion (O):

O — Patty drew the prettier flowers.

O — I drew the prettier flowers.

F — Val drew three purple birds.

F — The teacher said they were all very nice.

O — Blue is prettier than yellow.

O — All the pictures are the wrong color.

Write one fact about this story.
answers will vary

Write one opinion about this story.
answers will vary

©1995 Kelley Wingate Publications, Inc.   72   KW 1012

Answer Key

Name _____ skill: comprehension
Read the story.

Swimming

Swimming in my pool is better than swimming in a lake! My pool is in my back yard. I have to have Mom or Dad drive me to the lake. My pool is not as deep as the lake. I have some steps to sit on in my pool. The lake has a sandy beach to sit on. I do not like sand in my swimsuit. I am happy that I have such a nice pool. It is much better than any lake.

Tell whether each sentence is a fact (F) or an opinion (O):

O A pool is better than a lake.

F My pool is at my house.

O The lake is too deep.

F I can sit on the steps in my pool.

O The sand is not very nice to sit on.

F My pool makes me happy.

Write one fact about this story.

Answers will vary.

Write one opinion about this story.

Answers will vary.

©1995 Kelley Wingate Publications, Inc.   73   KW 1012

Name _____ skill: comprehension
Read the story.

Fall Leaves

Fall is the best season of all. In the summer all the leaves are green. In the winter there are no leaves at all. In the fall the leaves turn orange, yellow, red, and brown. Later, when the leaves fall from the trees, we can rake them into big piles. I love to make one large pile and then jump into it. It is so much fun to land on a soft pile of leaves.

Tell whether each sentence is a fact (F) or an opinion (O):

O Fall is better than summer or winter.

F In fall the leaves turn colors.

F Leaves fall from the trees in the fall season.

F We can rake the leaves into big piles.

O Raking leaves is a lot of fun.

O Leaves are pretty when they change colors.

Write one fact about this story.

Answers will vary.

Write one opinion about this story.

Answers will vary.

©1995 Kelley Wingate Publications, Inc.   74   KW 1012

Name _____ skill: blends

Using the first two letters in each word below, write each word in the correct column.

blue	sleep	clock	slow
clue	slap	black	blend
slip	climb	blind	clown
clan	blank	slope	bleed
clean	slab	class	slipper
block	slam	cloud	bloom

bl	sl	cl
blue	slip	clue
block	sleep	clan
blank	slap	clean
black	slab	climb
blind	slam	clock
blend	slope	class
bleed	slow	cloud
bloom	slipper	clown

THINK AHEAD: Can you find another bl, sl, and cl word?

bl _____ sl _____ cl _____

©1995 Kelley Wingate Publications, Inc.   75   KW 1012

Name _____ skill: blends

Using the first two letters from each word below, write each word in the correct column.

ship	slump	shot	slur
star	shut	stamp	stump
slim	shoot	stem	stir
shall	slap	sled	slit
shoe	stain	sheep	slat
shack	stall	sling	sting

st	sh	sl
star	ship	slim
stain	shall	slump
stall	shoe	slap
stamp	shack	sled
stem	shut	sling
stump	shoot	slur
stir	shot	slit
sting	sheep	slat

THINK AHEAD: Can you find another st, sh, and sl word?

st _____ sh _____ sl _____

©1995 Kelley Wingate Publications, Inc.   76   KW 1012

Answer Key

Name _____ skill: blends

Using the first two letters in each word below, write each word in the correct column.

crow	true	from	crown
frock	trick	frog	trash
crumb	tree	fruit	cram
trunk	cream	critter	frame
train	track	freeze	crook
trace	crew	friend	free

tr	fr	cr
trunk	frock	crow
train	from	crumb
trace	frog	cream
true	fruit	crew
trick	freeze	critter
tree	friend	crown
track	frame	cram
trash	free	crook

THINK AHEAD: Can you find another tr, fr, and cr word?

tr _____ fr _____ cr _____

©1995 Kelley Wingate Publications, Inc.   77   KW 1012

Name _____ skill: blends

Use the words in the list below to make three groups of words. Write the words that end in "ck" or "sh" in the first two columns. Find the third group by looking at the last two letters of the remaining words. Label the third column with these two letters. Write the words in this column.

fish	tack	nick	flash
first	fast	wash	last
trick	chick	list	wish
check	trash	nest	mash
east	chuck	truck	mush
dish	west	track	cast

ck	sh	st
truck	fish	first
check	dish	last
tack	trash	fast
chick	wash	west
chuck	flash	list
nick	wish	nest
trick	mash	last
track	mush	cast

THINK AHEAD: Can you find another ck, sh, and **st** word?

tr _____ fr _____ ___ _____

©1995 Kelley Wingate Publications, Inc.   78   KW 1012

Name _____ skill: blends

Use the words in the list below to make three groups of words. Write the words that begin with "str" or "squ" in the first two columns. Find the third group by looking at the first three letters of the remaining words. Label the third column with these three letters. Write the words in this column.

straw	squash	scream	squish
string	scram	strum	scrap
squirrel	strap	squiggle	scrape
scroll	squid	script	stripe
squall	strand	stream	scramble
squander	scribble	squabble	strut

str	squ	scr
straw	squirrel	scroll
string	squall	scram
strap	squander	scribble
strand	squash	scream
strum	squid	script
stream	squiggle	scrap
stripe	squabble	scrape
strut	squish	scramble

THINK AHEAD: Can you find another str, squ , and **scr** word?

str_____ squ _____ ___ _____

©1995 Kelley Wingate Publications, Inc.   79   KW 1012

Name _____ skill: blends

Use the words in the list below to make three groups of words. Write the words that begin with "ch" or "sh" in the first two columns. Find the third group by looking at the first two letters of the remaining words. Label the third column with these two letters and write the words in the column.

thin	shine	chair	share
think	choose	chin	should
thank	thunder	chain	shiny
cheese	child	shut	thimble
thistle	shell	shed	chat
thug	thigh	shoot	cheer

ch	sh	th
cheese	shine	thin
choose	shell	think
child	shut	thank
chair	shed	thistle
chin	shoot	thug
chain	share	thunder
chat	should	thigh
cheer	shiny	thimble

THINK AHEAD: Can you find another ch, sh , and **th** word?

ch _____ sh _____ ___ _____

©1995 Kelley Wingate Publications, Inc.   80   KW 1012

©1995 Kelley Wingate Publications, Inc.   127   CD-3709

Answer Key

Name _____   skill: blends

Use the words in the list below to make three groups of words. Write the words that begin with "dr" in the first column. Label the remaining two columns by looking at the first two letters of the left over words. Write the words in the correct columns.

price	draw	prom	tree
prod	droop	trim	trance
troop	dream	proof	drip
prune	prime	drop	track
treat	prank	drape	dram
trick	drool	trot	prim

dr	pr	tr
draw	price	troop
droop	prod	treat
dream	prune	trick
drool	prime	trim
drop	prank	trot
drape	prom	tree
drip	proof	trance
dram	prim	track

THINK AHEAD: Can you find another dr, pr, and tr word?

dr _____ __ _____ __ _____

©1995 Kelley Wingate Publications, Inc.   81   KW 1012

Name _____   skill: blends

Use the words in the list below to make three groups of words. Write the words that begin with "br" in the first column. Label the remaining two columns by looking at the first two letters of the left over words. Write the words in the correct columns.

bright	green	brick	from
froth	grit	brought	bring
gross	frog	fry	grab
grope	broke	frail	freak
grew	grow	branch	frost
brunch	grunt	brat	frank

br	fr	gr
bright	froth	grass
brunch	frog	grope
broke	fry	grew
brick	frail	green
brought	from	grit
branch	freak	grow
brat	frost	grunt
bring	frank	grab

THINK AHEAD: Can you find another br, fr, and gr word?

br _____ __ _____ __ _____

©1995 Kelley Wingate Publications, Inc.   82   KW 1012

Name _____   skill: blends

Use the words in the list below to make three groups of words. Write the words that end in "ch" in the first column. Label the remaining two columns by looking at the last two letters of the left over words. Write the words in the correct columns.

dent	bent	blind	bind
which	bend	inch	itch
blend	bunt	vent	latch
switch	brand	meant	lint
sand	bench	pond	lunch
land	mint	bunch	mount

ch	nt	nd
which	dent	blend
switch	bent	sand
bench	bunt	land
inch	mint	bend
bunch	vent	brand
itch	meant	blind
latch	lint	pond
lunch	mount	bind

THINK AHEAD: Can you find another ch, nt, and nd word?

ch _____ __ _____ __ _____

©1995 Kelley Wingate Publications, Inc.   83   KW 1012

Name _____   skill: decoding

Use the words in the list below to make three groups of words. Label the three columns by looking at the first letters of each word. Write the words in the correct columns.

glass	flop	glow	stream
strand	glum	flower	gloomy
flank	strong	flunk	stroll
streak	glad	flip	glint
strum	flour	glue	flap
strive	fleece	glove	struck

gl	str	fl
glass	strand	flank
glum	streak	flop
glad	strum	flour
glow	strive	fleece
glue	strong	flower
glove	stream	flunk
gloomy	stroll	flip
glint	struck	flap

THINK AHEAD: Can you find another word for each group?

_____ __ _____ __ _____

©1995 Kelley Wingate Publications, Inc.   84   KW 1012

Answer Key

©1995 Kelley Wingate Publications, Inc.

Name _____ skill: decoding

Use the words in the list below to make three groups of words. Label the three columns by looking at the last two letters of each word. Write the words in the correct columns.

fist	host	pink	plank
struck	stack	tank	back
toast	sank	buck	mast
stuck	sunk	rust	dunk
must	tack	ink	first
cluck	clock	sink	dust

st	ck	nk
first	struck	sank
toast	stuck	sunk
must	cluck	pink
host	stack	tank
rust	tack	ink
mast	clock	sink
fist	buck	plank
dust	back	dunk

THINK AHEAD: Can you find another word for each group?

_____ _____ _____

©1995 Kelley Wingate Publications, Inc. 85 KW 1012

Name _____ skill: r controlled vowels

Use the words in the list below to make three groups of words. Write the words with "ar" or "ir", or "ur" in the correct columns.

card	bird	burn	first
turn	harp	girl	far
nurse	sir	purse	star
arm	shirt	skirt	spark
hurt	barn	curb	curve
birth	curtain	circle	market

ar	ir	ur
card	birth	turn
arm	bird	nurse
harp	sir	hurt
barn	shirt	curtain
far	girl	burn
star	skirt	purse
spark	circle	curb
market	first	curve

THINK AHEAD: Can you find another word for each group?

_____ _____ _____

©1995 Kelley Wingate Publications, Inc. 86 KW 1012

Name _____ skill: r controlled vowels

Use the words in the list below to make three groups of words. Write the words with "or" or "er" in the first two columns. Label the third column by looking at the letters of the remaining words. Write these words in the column.

garden	over	dart	corn
paper	word	diver	part
term	large	color	herd
horn	bar	pork	fern
morning	perch	tarp	torn
tar	tart	germ	cord

or	er	ar
horn	paper	garden
morning	term	tar
word	over	large
color	perch	bar
pork	diver	tart
corn	germ	dart
torn	herd	tarp
cord	fern	part

THINK AHEAD: Can you find another word for each group?

_____ _____ _____

©1995 Kelley Wingate Publications, Inc. 87 KW 1012

Name _____ skill: r controlled vowels

Use the words in the list below to make three groups of words. Write the words with "ur" in the first column. Label the remaining columns by looking at the left over words. Write the words in the correct columns.

curl	yarn	fur	cork
fork	harm	form	bark
lurk	march	purr	fort
spur	motor	start	odor
murky	orange	cart	jar
burr	organ	curd	sugar

ur	or	ar
curl	fork	yarn
lurk	motor	harm
spur	orange	march
murky	organ	start
burr	form	cart
fur	cork	bark
purr	fort	jar
curd	odor	sugar

THINK AHEAD: Can you find another word for each group?

ur _____ _____ _____

©1995 Kelley Wingate Publications, Inc. 88 KW 1012

Answer Key

Name _____ skill: long vowels

Use the words in the list below to make three groups of words. Each group should have the same vowel sound. Write the words in the correct columns.

bike	side	beet	save
beam	tame	hate	bean
time	neat	line	mane
base	seem	name	fine
team	mice	nine	male
meat	case	hive	lean

long a	long e	long i
base	beam	bike
tame	team	time
case	meat	side
hate	neat	mice
name	seem	line
save	beet	nine
mane	bean	hive
male	lean	fine

THINK AHEAD: Can you find another word for each group?

_____ _____ _____

©1995 Kelley Wingate Publications, Inc.   89   KW 1012

Name _____ skill: long vowels

Use the words in the list below to make three groups of words. Each group should have the same vowel sound. Write the words in the correct columns.

tube	shave	ruby	nose
tale	tone	mate	tune
bone	lane	cute	cone
mute	lone	lame	duty
fate	note	rule	globe
wage	June	wave	boat

long o	long u	long a
bone	tube	tale
tone	mute	fate
lone	June	wage
note	ruby	shave
nose	cute	lane
cone	rule	mate
globe	tune	lame
boat	duty	wave

THINK AHEAD: Can you find another word for each group?

_____ _____ _____

©1995 Kelley Wingate Publications, Inc.   90   KW 1012

Name _____ skill: short vowels

Use the words in the list below to make three groups of words. Each group should have the same vowel sound. Write the words in the correct columns.

jam	ill	fed	tell
tan	sit	fill	ten
jack	get	van	fish
send	will	end	land
sat	bill	pal	vent
pin	neck	sad	

short a	short e	short i
jam	send	pin
tan	get	ill
jack	neck	sit
sat	fed	will
van	end	bill
pal	tell	fill
sad	ten	fish
land	vent	bit

THINK AHEAD: Can you find another word for each group?

_____ _____ _____

©1995 Kelley Wingate Publications, Inc.   91   KW 1012

Name _____ skill: short vowels

Use the words in the list below to make three groups of words. Each group should have the same vowel sound. Write the words in the correct columns.

odd	add	but	lap
cup	bad	cot	fun
dot	pond	sun	tap
not	cut	lot	and
jug	last	dog	fuss
man	pat	buff	log

short o	short u	short a
odd	cup	man
dot	jug	and
not	cut	bad
pond	but	last
cot	sun	pat
lot	buff	lap
dog	fun	tap
log	fuss	add

THINK AHEAD: Can you find another word for each group?

_____ _____ _____

©1995 Kelley Wingate Publications, Inc.   92   KW 1012

©1995 Kelley Wingate Publications, Inc.   130   **CD-3709**

Answer Key

©1995 Kelley Wingate Publications, Inc.

Name _____ skill: long and short vowels

Use the words in the list below to make two groups of words. Each group should have words with either long vowel sounds or short vowel sounds. Write the words in the correct columns.

teach	pint	take	glad
can	cent	see	sum
pal	poke	wind	fire
beat	true	tall	home
son	nut	hole	ate
new	bed	made	hat

Long Vowel Words   **Short Vowel Words**

teach	see	can	bed
beat	hole	pal	wind
pint	made	son	tall
poke	fire	new	glad
true	home	cent	sum
take	ate	nut	hat

THINK AHEAD: Can you find another word for each group?

_____ _____

©1995 Kelley Wingate Publications, Inc.   93   KW 1012

Name _____ skill: long and short vowels

Use the words in the list below to make two groups of words. Each group should have words with either long vowel sounds or short vowel sounds. Write the words in the correct columns.

woke	date	use	shut
twin	wig	pile	nose
rug	bake	duck	mate
drag	fell	kick	kite
dive	hid	cone	coat
mop	tape	pin	nap

Long Vowel Words   **Short Vowel Words**

woke	pile	twin	hid
dive	cone	rug	duck
date	nose	drag	kick
bake	mate	mop	pin
tape	kite	wig	shut
use	coat	fell	nap

THINK AHEAD: Can you find another word for each group?

_____ _____

©1995 Kelley Wingate Publications, Inc.   94   KW 1012

Name _____ skill: synonyms

Read the story below. Rewrite the story by replacing each underlined word with a word from the list that means about the same thing.

Anita's Party

Anita is <u>having</u> a party. We <u>should</u> take a <u>present</u>. We will <u>put on</u> some <u>pretty</u> hats and play games. <u>After</u> we eat the cake it will be time to <u>go home</u>.

beautiful	following	gift	giving
leave	must		wear

Anita is giving a party.
We must give a gift.
We will wear some beautiful
hats and play games. Following
the cake it will be time to
leave.

Draw a picture of the story.

©1995 Kelley Wingate Publications, Inc.   95   KW 1012

Name _____ skill: synonyms

Read the story below. Rewrite the story by replacing each underlined word with a word from the list that means about the same thing.

Toby

Toby is a <u>puppy</u>. He is <u>about</u> as <u>big</u> as a shoe box. He does not run <u>fast</u>. He is <u>slow</u>. He does not like to play with <u>very many</u> people. Toby is never <u>bad</u>. He does not <u>bite</u>. He <u>just</u> wants to be by himself!

almost	dog	large
lots of	naughty	nip
only	pokey	quickly

Toby is a dog. He is almost
as large as a shoe box. He
does not run quickly. He is
pokey. He does not like to play with
lots of people. Toby is never naughty.
He does not nip. He only wants to be by
himself.

Draw a picture of the story.

©1995 Kelley Wingate Publications, Inc.   96   KW 1012

Answer Key

Name _____ skill: synonyms

Read the story below. Rewrite the story by replacing each underlined word with a word from the list that means about the same thing.

A Hot Day

Today is hot. We had a drink of cold water. We cannot take a walk or throw a ball. We wear hats to make a shadow on our faces. Too much sun can make anyone sick. It is best to stay quiet on a day like this.

caps	cool	hike
ill	shade	sip
still	toss	warm

Today is warm. We had a sip of cool water. We cannot hike or toss a ball. We wear caps to make shade on our faces. Too much sun can make anyone ill. It is best to stay still on a day like this.

Draw a picture of the story.

©1995 Kelley Wingate Publications, Inc.   97   KW 1012

Name _____ skill: synonyms

Read the story below. Rewrite the story by replacing each underlined word with a word from the list that means about the same thing.

Peter and I

Peter is a six year old boy. His house is close to mine. We are good friends. Today we got wet with the hose. I smiled when he got my belly wet. We both laughed when the water splashed my mom!

giggled	grinned	home
lad	near	pals
soaked	squirted	stomach

Peter is a six year old lad. His home is near to mine. We are good pals. Today we got soaked with the hose. I grinned when he got my stomach wet. We both giggled when the water squirted my mom.

Draw a picture of the story.

©1995 Kelley Wingate Publications, Inc.   98   KW 1012

Name _____ skill: synonyms

Read the story below. Rewrite the story by replacing each underlined word with a word from the list that means about the same thing.

Mud

Few things are as much fun as getting dirty. First, pick a large black puddle to play in. Next, walk in. It is great to touch the mud around your toes. It feels good! When you are done you must wash up.

between	big	choose	clean	dark
enjoyable	feel	finished	muddy	not many
wade	wonderful			

Not many things are as enjoyable as getting muddy. First, choose a big dark puddle to play in. Next, wade in. It is great to feel the mud between your toes. It feels wonderful. When you are finished you must clean up.

Draw a picture of the story.

©1995 Kelley Wingate Publications, Inc.   99   KW 1012

Name _____ skill: synonyms

Read the story below. Rewrite the story by replacing each underlined word with a word from the list that means about the same thing.

A Bad Day

It was not a good day. I got up at sunrise and was tired all day. Mom forgot to iron my shirt. I ripped my pants. I lost my best two socks. I hit my arm as I hurried to school. I will be happy when this day is over!

arose	banged	dawn	glad
finished	nice	pair of	press
rushed	sleepy	tore	trousers

It was not a nice day. I arose at dawn and was sleepy all day. Mom forgot to press my shirt. I tore my trousers. I lost my best pair of socks. I banged my arm as I rushed to school. I will be glad when this day is finished.

Draw a picture of the story.

©1995 Kelley Wingate Publications, Inc.   100   KW 1012

Answer Key

Name _____   skill: synonyms

Read the story below. Rewrite the story by replacing each underlined word with a word from the list that means about the same thing.

The Yellow Taxi

The yellow <u>taxi</u> <u>rushed</u> <u>bravely</u> down the <u>busy</u> street. Its yellow paint was <u>shining</u> brightly in the evening sun. The cab <u>had</u> to <u>get to</u> the other side of the <u>city</u> before <u>sundown</u>. The ride <u>was over</u> as they <u>came to</u> the train station. That was not so <u>hard</u>!

arrived at	cab	crowded	difficult	dusk
ended	fearlessly	glowing	needed	reach
sped	town			

The yellow cab sped fearlessly down the crowded street. Its yellow paint was glowing brightly in the evening sun. The cab needed to reach the other side of the town before dusk. The ride ended as they arrived at the train station. That was not so difficult.

Draw a picture of the story.

©1995 Kelley Wingate Publications, Inc.   101   KW 1012

Name _____   skill: antonyms

Read the story below. Rewrite the story by replacing each underlined word with a word from the list that means the opposite.

Jody

Jody was <u>working</u> hard.
<u>She</u> was <u>pulling</u> <u>her</u> blocks <u>together</u>.
<u>She</u> put <u>a few</u> <u>on top of</u> the chair.
Jody built a <u>big</u> wall without using all of <u>her</u> blocks!

apart	he	he	little	many
his	playing	pushing	under	his

Jody was playing hard. He was pushing his blocks apart. He put many under the chair. Jody built a little wall without using all of his blocks.

Draw a picture of the story.

©1995 Kelley Wingate Publications, Inc.   102   KW 1012

Name _____   skill: antonyms

Read the story below. Rewrite the story by replacing each underlined word with a word from the list that means the opposite.

A New Pet

The little <u>girl</u> has <u>a new</u> pet.
It is a <u>black</u> dog with <u>soft</u> fur.
The <u>girl</u> has <u>many</u> pets that <u>run</u> <u>fast</u>.
<u>She</u> likes to play with them.

an old	slow	boy	few	he
slowly	walk	white	boy	hard

The little boy has an old pet. It is a white dog with hard fur. The boy has few pets that walk slowly. He likes to play with them.

Draw a picture of the story.

©1995 Kelley Wingate Publications, Inc.   103   KW 1012

Name _____   skill: antonyms

Read the story below. Rewrite the story by replacing each underlined word with a word from the list that means the opposite.

A Cold Drink

It was a <u>hot</u> <u>day</u>.
The <u>boy</u> was <u>standing</u> under a tree.
<u>He</u> wanted a <u>cold</u> drink of tea.
The <u>sun</u> began to <u>sink</u> in the sky.
<u>He</u> <u>quickly</u> <u>cooled</u> <u>down</u>.

cold	girl	hot	moon	night	rise	she
she	sitting	slowly	up	warmed		

It was a cold night. The girl was sitting under a tree. She wanted a hot drink of tea. The moon began to rise in the sky. She slowly warmed up.

Draw a picture of the story.

©1995 Kelley Wingate Publications, Inc.   104   KW 1012

Answer Key

Name _____ skill: antonyms

Read the story below. Rewrite the story by replacing each underlined word with a word from the list that means the opposite.

Jack
Jack the puppy has <u>a hard</u> job.
He must <u>learn</u> <u>many</u> things each <u>day</u>.
He must <u>walk</u> and <u>stay</u> when told.
He works with the same <u>boy</u> every <u>morning</u>.
The <u>hardest</u> job of all is to be <u>quiet</u> when he sees a cat.

an easy	easiest	evening	a few	girl
go	night	noisy	plays	run
teach				

Jack the puppy has an easy job. He must teach a few things each night. He must run and go when told. He works with the same girl every evening. The easiest job of all is to be noisy when he sees a cat.

Draw a picture of the story.

©1995 Kelley Wingate Publications, Inc.   105   KW 1012

Name _____ skill: antonyms

Read the story below. Rewrite the story by replacing each underlined word with a word from the list that means the opposite.

A Bad Day
Today was a <u>bad</u> day.
I <u>lost</u> my <u>left</u> shoe.
I was <u>late</u> for class and <u>last</u> in line.
I got all of my work <u>wrong</u>.
I almost <u>cried</u> because I was so <u>sad</u>.
<u>Tomorrow</u> <u>will be</u> a <u>better</u> day!

correct	early	first	found
good	happy	laughed	right
was	worse	yesterday	

Today was a good day. I found my right shoe. I was early for class and first in line. I got all of my work correct. I almost laughed because I was so happy. Yesterday was a worse day.

Draw a picture of the story.

©1995 Kelley Wingate Publications, Inc.   106   KW 1012

Name _____ skill: antonyms

Read the story below. Rewrite the story by replacing each underlined word with a word from the list that means the opposite.

Al and the Cat
Al was <u>brave</u> today.
<u>He</u> found a <u>thin</u>, <u>wild</u> cat that was <u>hungry</u>.
The cat <u>opened</u> its mouth.
Al put <u>his</u> hand <u>over</u> the cats face.
The cat licked Al with its <u>warm</u>, <u>rough</u> tongue.

closed	cool	fat	full
her	scared	she	smooth
tame	under		

Al was scared today. She found a fat, tame cat that was full. The cat closed its mouth. Al put her hand under the cat's face. The cat licked Al with its cool, smooth tongue.

Draw a picture of the story.

©1995 Kelley Wingate Publications, Inc.   107   KW 1012

Name _____ skill: antonyms

Read the story below. Rewrite the story by replacing each underlined word with a word from the list that means the opposite.

Sal
There was once a <u>strong</u> <u>man</u> named Sal.
<u>He</u> was <u>large</u> and very <u>tall</u>.
Sal could lift <u>many</u> <u>heavy</u> things <u>above</u> <u>his</u> shoulders.
On <u>winter</u> <u>mornings</u> at <u>sunrise</u> <u>he</u> liked to take long walks.
Sal would leave the house <u>before</u> it got <u>light</u> outside.

after	dark	evenings	few
light	she	short	summer
sunset	tiny	below	weak
woman	her	She	

There was once a weak woman named Sal. She was tiny and very short. Sal could lift few light things below her shoulders. On summer evenings at sunset she liked to take long walks. Sal would leave the house after it got dark outside.

Draw a picture of the story.

©1995 Kelley Wingate Publications, Inc.   108   KW 1012

Super Reader Award

_____

receives this award for

_____

Keep up the great work!

_____   _____

signed   date

Reading Award

_____

receives this award for

_____

Great Job!

_____   _____

signed   date

©1995 Kelley Wingate Publications, Inc.

CD-3709

also	asleep	bend	body
always	around	barn	bloom
air	apple	away	birthday
about	airways	awake	best

bush	circle	curb	does
breathe	chest	cover	dirt
brain	chair	could	dinner
box	cannot	cone	dance

energy	ears	dream	door
flower	fill	fall	every
hand	grow	fruit	flood
inside	hungry	have	hair

laces	look	mouth	near
job	long	magic	nap
jar	listen	lungs	must
invite	leap	love	movie

odd	not	nice	next
playground	place	piece	outside
rest	pretty	pot	please
share	send	safe	rope

sleep	someone	step	winner
skin	snack	spring	touch
side	smile	spin	think
shoes	small	special	strong